TASTING FOOD, TASTING FREEDOM

Excursions into Eating, Culture, and the Past

TASTING FOOD, TASTING FREEDOM

SIDNEY W. MINTZ

Beacon Press, Boston

Beacon Press
25 Beacon Street
Boston, Massachusetts 02108-2892
www.beacon.org

Beacon Press books
are published under the auspices of
the Unitarian Universalist Association of Congregations.

10   12 11 10

This book is printed on acid-free paper that meets the uncoated paper
ANSI/NISO specifications for permanence as revised in 1992.

Text design by Iris Weinstein

Composition by Wilsted & Taylor Publishing Services

Library of Congress Cataloging-in-Publication Data

Mintz, Sidney Wilfred, 1922–
Tasting food, tasting freedom : excursions into eating, culture, and
the past / by Sidney W. Mintz.
p.   cm.
Includes bibliographical references and index
ISBN 978-0-8070-4629-6 (pbk.)
1. Food habits. 2. Diet. 3. Food—Philosophy. 4. Eating
(Philosophy) I. Title.
GT2850.M58   1996
394.1—dc20   95-47569

To my sisters Alice and Vivian
and to the memory of Evelyn
and to their husbands
Eli, Sid, and Morrie

Grace to Be Said at the Supermarket

That God of ours, the Great Geometer,
Does something for us here, where He hath put
  (if you want to put it that way) things in shape,
Compressing the little lambs in orderly cubes,
Making the roast a decent cylinder,
Fairing the ellipsoid of a ham,
Getting the luncheon meat anonymous
In squares and oblongs with the edges beveled
Or rounded (streamlined, maybe, for greater speed).

Praise Him, He hath conferred aesthetic distance
Upon our appetites, and on the bloody
Mess of our birthright, our unseemly need,
Imposed significant form. Through Him the brutes
Enter the pure Euclidean kingdom of number,
Free of their bulging and blood-swollen lives
They come to us holy, in cellophane
Transparencies, in the mystical body,

That we may look unflinchingly on death
As the greatest good, like a philosopher should.

HOWARD NEMEROV

Contents

Preface   xi

1. Introduction   1
2. Food and Its Relationship to
   Concepts of Power   17
3. Tasting Food, Tasting Freedom   33
4. The Conquest of Honey by Sucrose   50
5. Sugar and Morality   67

6. Color, Taste, and Purity   84

7. Cuisine: High, Low, and Not at All   92

8. Eating American   106

Notes   125

Works Cited   135

Index   145

Preface

My father was a cook. One of my sisters corrected me for years, insisting that he was a restaurateur. But I know that he was a cook. Only by the oddest of routes—the sort people made rootless by circumstance must sometimes take—did he arrive at cooking for a living.

When my parents, not yet married, reached New York City from the village slums of eastern Europe at the start of this century, my father, Shlomo ("Solomon") Mintz, was a diemaker, freshly discharged from the Czarist army, after six years' service in a signal battalion. My mother, Fromme Leah ("Fannie") Mintz, who had been in the Bund, a Jewish socialist organization sternly proscribed by the Czarist government, became a seamstress in a New York sweatshop. Soon enough she joined the Industrial Workers of the World, or "Wobblies," as they were called, as an organizer in the New York garment trade. Her parents did not approve and the job did not pay well.

Nor did men's work. According to my father, diemaking was paying $3.50 a week in New York City in 1901. He took a job as a clothing salesman on Canal Street, working for a distant relative, and apparently hated every minute of it. But that is a different story.

When my parents decided to get married—they were first (cross) cousins, and it was a common Ashkenazic practice—my mother made emigration to a small town far from New York City a precondition, saying that she didn't want to raise children in a city. In response my father wrote to an old army friend, Ben Dorfman, who at that time was washing dishes in a diner in Dover, New Jersey. Ben, an orphan, had played the tuba in the military band quartered in the same divisional headquarters as my father's signal corps battalion.

They were a strange pair. My father was not much interested in books, words, or most ideas, while Ben was interested in little else; but they were close friends. As it turned out, the owner of the diner needed a dishwasher on the night shift. My father left his Canal Street haberdashery sales job, and joined Ben Dorfman at the sink, in Dover.

After their wedding in New York—my mother was ashamed to invite any of her IWW comrades because marriage was a bourgeois institution—my parents took the train to Dover, and a horse and carriage from the train station to their new home, a rented house, with Ben Dorfman as a permanent houseguest. He stayed with us until he died of cancer, during my childhood. Dover, New Jersey, is where my siblings and I were born and grew up.

It was perhaps ten years after my parents moved there that the owner of the Lackawanna House—the diner, that is—bought a Ferris wheel, sold the diner to Ben Dorfman and my father, and went off with a carnival. I know that sounds made up, but it isn't, at least not by me. Ben and my father, who had both been saving money since my father moved to Dover, ran the diner until they were able to replace it by building a big restaurant and hotel. How they came to that course of action I never learned, but it coincided almost perfectly with the sinking of the *Lusitania* and U.S. entry into World War I. Since Dover, New Jersey, was blessed by having both a government arsenal and a powder works in nearby towns, the restaurant and hotel business flourished, and my father became a restaurateur, just like that sister kept telling me. He also became convinced that he was a financial genius. He remained a restaurateur until about 1929, when he lost his shirt, along with everyone else. Overnight, he became a cook, but now he was back to a diner again. He remained a cook almost until the day he died.

I barely remember him as a restaurateur, but I came to know him well as a cook. I ate most of my meals in the diner; and it retained the name of the Lackawanna House. My father would make my "lunch" during the summer months when, home from college, I worked swing shift at the nearby arsenal. We had twenty minutes to eat, from 4:00 A.M. until 4:20 A.M., and in that time I would matter-of-factly consume the two sandwiches, two pieces of fruit, and thermos of coffee he packed for me each evening. Around 8:20 A.M., I would arrive exhausted from work once more at the diner, and after a few minutes' respite on the floor, I would be seized by gnawing hunger and help myself to a proper breakfast. That usually meant a large glass of freshly squeezed orange juice, three fried eggs over lightly, a ham steak, a grilled banana, toast, and coffee. My father, who would arrive around 11:00 A.M. (by which time I was comfortably asleep at home), is reported to have complained regularly that our financial security as a family would remain at risk until I moved out or lost my appetite.

My father did not like my mother's cooking and competed with her quite nastily whenever she tried to cook. But it would have been surprising had she been able to cook better than he, since she could do practically everything else better. She spoke and wrote English much better; she was excellent at arithmetic, and he was not; her powers of reasoning were clearly superior. My father, in contrast, was a superb gardener; he had unusual mechanical abilities; and he was—I think—a great cook. He was also a profoundly sensual man.

My mother's attitude toward food differed entirely from his. She was a spiritual creature, in her own way. Her consciousness was so preempted by political affairs that she scarcely knew what she was eating, and cared less. Rosie Isadorczyk, one of the waitresses, used to say that Fannie's idea of a good meal was a cup of black coffee and an editorial in the *Freiheit* (a left-wing Yiddish newspaper). In contrast, my father loved birds, animals, women, babies, and melody. He liked the feel of leather. He played the ocarina, danced the *Kazatski*, and sang beautifully. He collected and repaired cuckoo clocks; there were dozens of them in our house. For years he carried around with him a tiny bit of that fine sandpaper called crocus cloth, with which he polished the oaken panels in the foyer of the house until they shone with a cathedral-like light. He was not interested in intellectualizing anything; quite the contrary. He distrusted words and believed in feelings. My mother's indifference to food filled him with emotions akin to horror. She would quite innocently read the newspaper while dining on a plate of cold cooked turnips, then complain bitterly of indigestion afterward. On being told what she had eaten to produce this effect, he would look as pained as he was repelled.

My father's approach to food was idiosyncratic, but basically convincing. He had, after all, learned to cook only by watching the people who, over the years, had cooked for him. Toward the end of his career as a restaurateur—the truly bad years, when he still had a big establishment, but no customers in it and no liquid capital at all—he hired a Chinese cook to "attract business." It was as ill-fated a move as any other, for there was no business to attract. People had no money and did not eat out. Cheng Dai Mo, the Chinese cook, was anxious to return to China, hoping to become a pilot in Chiang Kai-shek's air force; but he hung around for a year or so, during which time my father learned all that he could about Dai Mo's cooking. When Dai Mo finally quit—there were no customers, and he must have been paid a pittance—my father continued for some time thereafter to advertise his oriental cuisine. Somewhere in the family trash, there is a photo of him, taken by his friends. He is wearing his chef's hat and smiling at the camera. Someone has written in ink above his head "Sol Min, Chinese cook." His finesse in this culinary sphere was pitiable. People would bring him fresh noodles from New York's Chinatown, which he would deep fry; he added MSG (called then "epicurean powder") to his chicken soup; he learned to make egg foo yung and some version of that appalling dish called chop suey, and a noodle and chicken soup combination I knew as yat gaw min. Clearly, my father's expertise as a chef lay in other directions.

I remember in particular his soups: sorrel soup, made with fresh sorrel, sour cream, hard-boiled egg, and scallions; *kapusta*, made with slightly fermented cabbage, brisket of beef, tomatoes, and the spectacular dried Russian *Boletus*, called *grbi*; beet *borscht* and meat *borscht*; clam chowder (both versions of which represented a sharp turn away from the food of his immediate ancestors); *kholodnik*, "the little cold one," his name for a traditional Polish soup made with fresh garden vegetables, sour salt (citric acid), and boiled dilled and buttered potatoes steaming on the side; lamb and barley soup; white (marrow fat) bean and ham bone soup; oxtail soup—they were all unexpectedly rich because of his intensely concentrated stocks. So, too, were his stews and steaks. He would cook anything from any animal. He made a marvelous kidney stew, and I became quite fond of a peppery lung stew he created. We ate kidneys, oxtail, sandwiches of marrow and black bread, brains. His french fries were excellent, but he hated to make them because he thought they were indigestible. When a customer ordered them, he was wont to come out of the kitchen wiping his hands on his apron, in order to lecture the unfortunate client on the error of his ways. (Some customers said his was the only restaurant in the world where the customer was always wrong.)

He favored smoked fish, as do so many people from eastern and northern Europe. We had a bit of herring to start each meal. I once complained about the herring because invariably it was there. "Don't make fun of the herring," he said. "If there hadn't been any herring, there wouldn't have been any Jews." I recognized instantly what he meant. The rural poor of eastern Europe were chronically starved for animal protein. A piece of chicken, perhaps once a month, was supplemented by the herring; dried beans probably supplied most of the protein they got. Doing fieldwork on Puerto Rican sugarcane plantations fifteen or so years later, I learned to enjoy the stewed red beans or pigeon peas served over white rice, and flavored with coriander, garlic, and perhaps a sliver of smoked pork—the herring's equivalent. Years later an anthropological colleague talked about his Irish grandfather describing what he called a "famous Irish dish" named "potatoes and point." One boiled up a pot of potatoes, then hung a bit of salt pork on a string over the table. Then one stuck one's fork in the potato, pointed it at the salt pork, and ate the potato. I learned over the years that, except for the vegetarian regions, poor people the world over had suffered from the same lack of animal protein; most poor people in the world today still do. But my first lesson about it came from my father.

Though he had been raised in an average Jewish home—we would probably say "orthodox" now—just before the start of this century, my father had turned his back on religion while still an adolescent and quarreled violently with his father. (I suspect that he was influenced by the enlightenment movement among east European Jews called the Haskalah, but I do not really know that.) His food habits revealed how firm the break had been. He learned to eat and to cook shellfish, to mix milk and meat, to forgo the separation of dishes and silverware, to enjoy pork (which he cooked marvelously well) in its many variant forms. He never made his children eat anything they did not want, but he did coax us to *taste* everything he made. A sound practice—for the next time he cooked the dish, it would seem less exotic and much more appetizing. He thus successfully raised four children, all of whom became gluttons (and several, good cooks) and none of whom has an allergy to any food (except me, at times, to clams).

He ate sparingly himself, hated deep-fried foods, and leaned toward the kind of diet now popular with young middle-class people—no red meat, little fat of any kind, lots of fruits and vegetables steamed or boiled, substantial complex carbohydrates (including such "lost" foods as buckwheat groats, lentils, and barley), and no foods to which sugar was added. He ate lots of dairy foods and eggs—they had not yet been found wanting—and he said that the medical insistence that he give up salt near the end of his life proved to be the worst burden he'd ever had, a far harder chore than forgoing cigarettes. At times, after having cooked for his growing family—by then, and with in-laws and grandchildren, some twenty of us, all told—a six-course dinner starting with a handsome hors d'oeuvre and ending with home-baked cakes and pies, he would join us at table with his own meal. It usually consisted of a toasted bagel, cream cheese, a sliced tomato, sprinkled with dill or basil, and some smoked salmon or whitefish or salmon caviar. My sister Ev would exclaim, "Goddamn it, no matter what you give us, what *you* eat always looks better!"

We drank at every meal but breakfast: beer with certain dishes, but a shot of whiskey—sometimes two—before each lunch and dinner. I was put on that regimen when I could not have been more than about ten years old. He viewed this dose of whiskey—he called it *schnapps*—as a healthful stimulant to appetite. There was absolutely no negative feeling in my family about drinking. The first time I got drunk was at age eight, on Passover wine, and I recall my mother thought it pretty funny, as we walked home from her parents' house. But my parents felt a profound horror of alcoholism. My father would not serve alcohol in the restaurant before Prohibition. After its repeal, and once he was installed in the diner, he felt he had no choice. But he hated to deal with people who were drunk. I can remember him on occasions sobering up some over-refreshed customer in the diner with a whiff of newly grated horseradish.

When I was about eleven, my father came down with a bad case of shingles. He was quite unable to cook, and I was sent to him so he could tell me how to do it. It turned out that I was going to prepare a vast quantity of tomato sauce and meat balls. He gave me instructions, which I carefully recorded, and then I went into the kitchen and followed the instructions. I cannot remember now why I, rather than someone else, was chosen—but it was probably just for my benefit. I can remember the wave of solid satisfaction I felt from cooking this food. It was not easy for me to please my father at anything, but this time I felt reassured that he was hinting he could depend on me.

My attitudes toward food, and my esteem for it, come from my father. This book would never have been written but for him. My best memories of him are associated indissolubly with the kitchen. He didn't think much of me in the kitchen, to be sure. He would watch me carving a standing rib and would say: "How is it that you have a Ph.D. and you still can't carve a standing rib?" I imagine that he is up there now, looking down, and saying to his friends, "Look, there's my son. He makes his living *writing* about food!"

I n writing this book, which includes several new essays and some previously published papers, I benefited from the help of many friends and colleagues. I thank them all: Jeff Brooks, Sid Cantor, Elizabeth Dunn, Harriet Friedmann, Enrique García Galiano, Ashraf Ghani, Judy Goldstein, Jerry Hagelberg, Françoise Héritier, Jeff Horn, Phil McMichael, Luciene

Pisa, Paul Rozin, J. B. Schneewind, Rebecca Scott, Brita Servaes, Dale Tomich, Immanuel Wallerstein, John Walton, Eric Wolf, the editors of *Etnofoor*, the Wenner-Gren Foundation, and the Collège de France. As always, Marge Collignon has done yeoman work in putting the manuscript in order, not once but repeatedly, tracking down efficiently those things I managed to misplace, throw away, or file incorrectly. Also, as always, all of my colleagues in anthropology, and our students, give meaning to one's life as a teacher and as a learner. They make "book-writing" fun.

"Pa koké makout," say the Haitians, "pi ro pasé mê ou." Don't hang your basket higher than you can reach. I forgot that advice while working with these essays, and a number of kind persons did what they could to rescue me from my own hubris. I am grateful to Nancy Harmon Jenkins for her astute eye, and to Darrell Corti for incisive questions. My colleague and chair, Gillian Feeley-Harnik, provided acute observations on many parts of the text, and much enlightenment during our frequent talks about food. Ann Finkbeiner generously agreed to make a rapid reading of the penultimate draft, and gave me the benefit of her critical acumen. I am grateful to Lindee Chin, who prepared the index with her characteristic celerity and intelligence. Deb Chasman of Beacon Press has worked with me fruitfully for some years now, and it was she who gently but decisively nudged me toward the cobbling together of so many scraps. My wife, Jackie, never fails to give me reassurance, strengthened by both good taste and absolutely dependable criticism. She has had to read some of these essays too many times. For persisting errors, both of fact and of judgment, it is my cruel misfortune to have nobody but myself to blame.

chapter one
INTRODUCTION

In his first book, *The Palm-Wine Drinkard*, the Nigerian writer Amos Tutuola [1953] introduced his readers to a set of mythical characters, all of whom are described by the chief character himself, a drunkard with an utterly insatiable thirst for palm wine. After other adventures, the palm-wine drunkard marries; the firstborn child of their union is born from his wife's thumb. This exceptional baby comes into the world already speaking like a ten-year-old and grows to more than three feet tall within an hour of his birth. But what is most remarkable about him is his eating behavior.

The little boy tells his parents his name is ZURRJIR ("which means a son who would change himself into another thing very soon" [1953, 32]), and he is endowed with a mighty appetite. He eats and eats and eats, and if people try to keep him from eating, he thrashes them and continues to eat. His strength is great, his appetite infinite:

> [A]s he had eaten all the food which had been prepared against the night, then we began to cook other food, but when it was the time to put the food down from the fire, he put it down for himself and at the same time, he began to eat that again as it was very hot, before we could stop him, he had eaten all the food and we tried all our best to take it from him, but we could not do it at all.
> [1953, 33]

This wayward son does much mischief besides. To get rid of him, the drunkard finally decides to burn his house down. The son is burned up, too, to everyone's vast relief. But his mother pokes around in the ashes to find a bauble she had forgotten, saying "and there I saw that the middle of the ashes rose up suddenly and at the same time there appeared a half-bodied baby, he was talking with a lower voice like a telephone" [1953, 35]. This half-baby with the voice like a telephone, whose name means something that will change into something else—what could he possibly represent? Whence this utterly insatiable hunger, in a baby born of a thumb, now reduced to a half-baby, his hunger unassuaged?

Tutuola has been analyzed by a score of literary critics, but the themes in this story do not seem frighteningly complex. Most of us have no difficulty imagining a desire, a *hunger*, so intense that it brooks no opposition. Nor is it difficult to conjure the thought of a hunger so painful that one might fight, even kill, in order to be able to satisfy it. And the voice like a telephone— we forget how different we sound on such devices because we are so used to them. But everyone is aware of the *modernity* that electronic media carry; a "lower voice like a telephone" sounds like life today. Changing from one thing to another is what so many wish, and indeed it does happen—but mostly we do not change into what we wish, but into something else. This book about rural Nigeria on the eve of independence lets us confront raging desire: an insatiable, aggressive appetite embodied in a powerful—indeed, indestructible—spirit. I think it sounds very modern.

I begin in this manner because what follows is a book about food, and so a book about hungers as well—hungers and their satisfaction. It is also a book about change, aspiring to link together through its themes the past with the present. To some extent, it is about the emergence of modernity, and what modern life has meant, in relation to food.

What was written about food and eating by anthropologists more than a century ago dealt mostly with feast and sacrifice—people's food relationships with their gods; with food taboos and injunctions, usually religious in nature; with the role of foods in how people were ranked socially; with cannibalism, and why people engaged in it (if, though some have denied it, they indeed did); more superficially, with foods considered by most Western cultures especially disagreeable, exotic, or repulsive.

Anthropologists who began to study such things in the field at the start of this century went from their own large, urban, Western societies to others, then still numerous, in which people were consuming foods they had produced (or gathered, or caught) themselves, most of them relying relatively little on distant exchanges for any important things that they ate. Women in such societies commonly did much of the labor to collect or grow food, as well as nearly all of the cooking. Most anthropologists were men, and didn't find such matters especially interesting. Hence it would probably be accurate to say that food and eating got much less attention in their own right as anthropological subjects than they really deserved. They were more interesting if they offended the observer, baffled him, or were ceremonialized, than if they simply pleased those who were doing the cooking and eating. Food was an instrument for the study of other things.

That it cemented loyalties, reminded people who they were in relation to others, fortified them for their tasks, and linked them to
their gods, were all known aspects of eating behavior, and these
features were studied. It was not the food or its preparation that
was of interest, so much as what, socially speaking, the food and
eating could be used for.

There were exceptions. One thinks, for instance of Franz
Boas's amazing volume of recipes (mostly but not only for
salmon), collected by George Hunt from the Kwakiutl people of
the Pacific Northwest [Boas 1921, 305–602]. But male anthropologists generally preferred to study war, initiation, trials by ordeal,
even kinship—over skinning rabbits, drying gutted salmon on
racks, beer-making, or pots and pans. Bronislaw Malinowski's
beautiful studies of the Trobriand Islanders, which brought together yam cultivation, feasting, magic, and chiefhood, were certainly much involved with food; but they were really concerned
with what food did for the social order.[1]

Underlying the rich symbolic universe that food and eating
always represent, however, there is the animal reality of our living existence. It is not separate from our humanity, but is an integral part of it. Only because most of us eat plentifully and frequently and have not known intense hunger may we sometimes
too easily forget the astonishing, at times even terrifying, importance of food and eating. That becomes clear as soon as we give
the subject of food a moment's serious thought. Without at least
minimal access to food and water, we die. Except for the struc-
turally determined irritability of all living matter and the organ-
ism's built-in drive to reproduce, nothing defines our nature as
living creatures more dramatically than our ingestion. A principal source of human suffering in the modern world is still—as it
has for so long been—hunger. Hunger, however, has many uses.
Fasting, for instance, is a dramatic means by which to discover
the power of food, as is obvious to anyone who has fasted for
even a single day. But people who fast for some larger good are
moved by a moral desire; they *will* against their own hunger. Be-

ing starved by someone else, as happens still to so many people, is a more dramatic—and demoralizing—way to discover hunger's terrible power.

Food is something we think about, talk about, conceptualize. But we more than abstract it and desire it—we really must consume it to stay alive. Our desire for it can grow far beyond anticipatory pleasure; desire can turn to pain. When we get some, we must put it inside our mouths to be processed there so that it can enter digestibly into our bodies. Because of the satisfaction of hunger, as well as for many other more complicated reasons, the feeling of eating can be intensely pleasurable.

Yet eating can also excite deep ambivalence because the act of eating seems so animal. That ambivalence has characteristic cultural markings: not all societies feel the same way about food, and the food itself can be many different things. People eat just about anything that won't kill them, and even a lot of things that will. Attitudes about food are just as varied: about even such basic things as what it means to eat; what eating has to do with being human; and what it means to eat properly.

A clear if extreme sign of human ambivalence about eating is revealed by the symptoms of food-related pathologies, such as anorexia and bulimia. Though these pathologies are by no means limited to the Western nations, they are far more common in the West than elsewhere, accompanying as they do an overabundance of food. They are also far more common among women than among men. One way to think of such infirmities is as strange kinds of overcompensation—not eating, even when hungry; or gorging, and then vomiting—overcompensation, that is, for the persistent desire that hunger excites. Being overcompensatory does not make them one whit less real torment to their sufferers. The ill are obsessed about food; they suffer over food. It is food, or what food means to them, that makes them sick. But what food means to them is itself a cultural product; that the principal sufferers of such illnesses should be young white Western middle-class females is a powerful cultural signal. If anorexics may be said to misperceive their own bodies, if they feel they must "punish" themselves accordingly, then that is food-related behavior. Similarly food-related is the feeling bulimics have that they must pay up for their inability to control rampant desire. But these conceptions of desirable but unachievable equilibrium, the moral investment that food and its rejection come to represent, the social structure of societies within which women of this status come to suffer in these ways, are distinctly culture-specific, not general to our species. Nourishment, a basic biological need, becomes something else because we humans transform it symbolically into a system of meaning for much more than itself. That seemingly needless overcomplication is a distinctively human undertaking, which every culture embraces, but each somewhat differently.

The propensity to expunge and suppress our "animal" need to eat (or at least to worry about it and verbalize it), somehow to inform it morally, is probably not universal. But it figures importantly in North American culture as a conscious, ever-present idea. Ingestion's consequences and its accompaniments, noises and smells, can be a source of social discomfort (at least for many Americans). The way people feel about such things varies from class to class, and from one ethnic group to another; but digestion must at least be treated as a source of humor, lest it be taken as seriously as it sometimes is. Earthy people and earthy cultures may vaunt how readily they accept bodily functions and dysfunctions as integral parts of our human natures; but in the West, at least, these things, whatever else they may be, are often seen as uncomfortable manifestations of our animality.

In the United States, other phenomena associated with food and eating have been aggravated in modern times by a compulsive concern with the way the body is seen and assessed. The extent of the individual's ability to control and manage and discipline the body—not in all societies can such verbs be applied so matter-of-factly—is considered a reflection on individual self-control. Every act of eating can thus be made into a test of will.

Since eating is morally colored, it is not surprising that half of the American people—and 90 percent of American women—are said to be on diets at any one time. To the extent that this is a gender-marked phenomenon, anorexia and bulimia may come to look like no more than merely the flip side of the self-constructed beautiful You.

From this example it should be clear that food and eating afford us a remarkable arena in which to watch how the human species invests a basic activity with social meaning—indeed, with so much meaning that the activity itself can almost be lost sight of. In the United States, the rituals of courtship afford a provocative instance. Several years ago I urged one of my students to write her term paper on the preparations young college females make before going on a dinner date with a male, and on the food-related behavior exhibited by males and females on such dates. There is no need here to review her findings at length: the meals covertly eaten *before* going out, and the oil drunk to slow or forestall intoxication; the remedies intended to prevent nausea, flatulence, or bad breath; the careful investments in posture and gesture to conceal, or to distract the eye of the other; the striking differences in food-related intent, as in the manner of "addressing" the food before one; and how culturally specific maleness and femaleness can be given solidity, by the different ways in which males and females behave around food. The paper gave real substance to the argument I mean to make here. If we were not human, things would be different. But if we weren't human, I wouldn't be writing this down.

For us humans, then, eating is never a "purely biological" activity (whatever "purely biological" means). The foods eaten have histories associated with the pasts of those who eat them; the techniques employed to find, process, prepare, serve, and consume the foods are all culturally variable, with histories of their own. Nor is the food ever simply eaten; its consumption is always conditioned by meaning. These meanings are symbolic, and communicated symbolically; they also have histories. These

are some of the ways we humans make so much more complicated this supposedly simple "animal" activity.

In one sense, the symbolic investment of meaning in food has
little to do with the food itself. I am reminded of a Beatles song
that tells of a cleaning woman in church, who cleans up the rice
thrown at a past wedding. To get from that rice to what the story
tells us is a long enough trip to make the specific character of the
food seem hardly relevant. But in fact what the food is, how
people come to have it, how it is prepared, whether it is plentiful
or scarce, under what circumstances it is available—all of these
circumstances, and many others, are integrated into what the
food means. This was the way the early anthropologists thought
about food, most of all; it continues to be what's most important
about it for anthropology.

No other fundamental aspect of our behavior as a species
except sexuality is so encumbered by *ideas* as eating; the entan-
glements of food with religion, with both belief and sociality,
are particularly striking. A familiar illustration involves those
peoples who first domesticated, then herded and cared for (and
lived off) the sheep. They were its shepherds for millennia; and
then one day the lamb of God became *their* shepherd. A particular god, at a particular time. The paschal sacrifice is a name for
Passover; the term "paschal" comes from the Hebrew word for
Passover; it is also the word meaning Easter. The paschal lamb is
the paschal sacrifice. The lamb of God died for our sins, we are
told. The Last Supper, the Eucharist, the Passover feast, suggest
the intricate mixing of food with belief. Here, crudely simplified,
are the kinds of associations early anthropologists recognized
and studied. There seems to be no end of them.

Ingestion and sexuality, both intimate manifestations of our
nature as living creatures, and equally remote in our case from
their roles in the lives of other species, stand in different but par-
allel relationships to our human consciousness. Their twin importance is revealed to some degree by their common equation
in popular language. The "coarse language" of everyman—in

which desire, substance, act, and satiation, whether in eating or in sex, may be described with the selfsame words—is still alive, despite the heavy taboos surrounding deliberate and poetically startling confusion. "It must be jelly, 'cause jam don't shake like that" is not considered Shakespearean prose. Because of their thinly veiled unity, sexual idioms in food's language are doubly discomfiting. Novelists, filmmakers, poets, and songwriters take common advantage of the fact that food and sexuality lie close together.

In contrast to the unending need for food, the sexual drive is subject to enormous cultural manipulation. To be sure, within limits, so is the need to eat—but only within limits that are frighteningly clear. In the case of mammalian behavior generally, sexual and food-seeking behavior are usually easy to distinguish: sexual activity is periodic, seasonal, hormonally regulated. Not, however, in the case of the human species; for human beings (and like hunger), sexuality is sempiternal. Yet these hungers are differently subject to social control, and are differently managed in different societies.

If we leave aside the food enthusiasts, ordinary mortals do not enshrine food in some special niche of the sort we save for love. People can—indeed, often do—have intense feelings about food, even those persons who have never been truly hungry. But they do not openly concede to food the deep importance they accord to love, and for obvious reasons: love has to do with other persons, in a different way from food. The ordinariness of food, its accessibility, our everyday need for it, and its physiological consequences may sometimes make it seem less important than it is. Yet food has a special status in our spectrum of sensory experience. The French sociologist Pierre Bourdieu [1984, 79] has suggested why, eloquently:

> It is probably in tastes in *food* that one would find the strongest and most indelible mark of infant learning, the lessons which longest withstand the distancing or col-

lapse of the native world and most durably maintain nostalgia for it. The native world is, above all, the maternal world, the world of primordial tastes and basic foods, of the archetypal relation to the archetypal cultural good, in which pleasure-giving is an integral part of pleasure and of the selective disposition towards pleasure which is acquired through pleasure.

I think that food remains an odd subject, at least in the United States, because its sensory power often conflicts so jarringly with our strangely disembodied, rather puritanical and very American, conceptions of ourselves.

Anthropologists have always been interested, at least in a general way, in how societies (especially nonmachine societies) provisioned themselves. Even though there were not many good early studies of how food was prepared, distributed, and eaten, there was a long-standing preoccupation with what needed to be done to keep the society functioning, and of course food figured centrally in answering that question. In the United States, anthropologists such as Otis T. Mason and Clark Wissler charted the lifeways of Native American peoples in terms of their basic subsistence, for example, and spoke of "salmon areas" and "maize areas" and "bison areas" in describing Indian life. But pioneer fieldworkers such as Boas and Malinowski dealt with societies that were economically more self-contained, at least so far as their traditional foods were concerned. In the last hundred years those economies have almost entirely disappeared. Anthropology today deals with a world in which, more and more, people do not consume what they produce and do not produce what they consume, even much of their food.

In this world, anthropologists have begun to think about international issues involving the differential food productivity of different continents, the spread of new foods, and especially, food supplies in relation to the growth of world population. Because food is, so to speak, the "bottom line" in maintaining life, and though famine has now become relatively rare, the world food picture is still immensely important politically; a news report on any troubled area is almost certain to touch on issues of food and food availability.

This is one of the fundamental ways in which food is now connected to issues of power. The connection is certainly not new. But some of the ways in which food and power are linked today are themselves new. People in distant lands now often decide by their actions who will continue living and who will have to die. Hardly any aspect of power could be more awful than that. Yet in the modern world this development is rarely recognized as power. The decisions are often collective and procedural, as in legislatures, say, ruling against foreign aid; or made by large corporations, deciding to produce their bananas on island A, and to stop producing them on island B. The result is that some people are likely to die; and neither they themselves, nor those who are responsible, know who killed them. The most profound ethical issues are raised by the assertion that every living human being has a sacred right to eat because decisions are being made all the time that—by their inevitable consequences—end up causing people to die of hunger. Establishing the linkages between such decision-making and its victims, exposing those linkages so that the decision-making itself becomes ethically visible, may be a task remote from anthropology's older concerns. But it is well worth any anthropologist's time today.

Such linkages can be studied historically, and many anthropologists have learned from social historians how they can reveal the political and economic significance of past events connected to food. Though not his central theme, when Redcliffe Salaman wrote *The History and Social Influence of the Potato* [1949], he devoted considerable space to the Irish potato famine or "Great Hunger" of 1845–49. Cecil Woodham-Smith, in *The Great Hunger* [1962], made that catastrophe her particular subject: a million dead, another million who emigrated, all because of a diseased crop. The potato itself, that strange member of the deadly nightshade family, had been imported to Europe from the New World where it was first domesticated. Because it was finally turned into the principal nutritive mainstay of the Irish people, the potato had a leading role in the tragedy. But this was not the potato's fault; it was a man-made tragedy. The power both of the landowners and of the state entered actively into the story. The near-total dependence of the people on one single food and the unpreparedness of the state to assist them were both aspects of Irish colonial history. The potatoes merely rotted; but too little was done by the society's rulers to avert the disaster, once the tragic dependence of an entire people on a single crop had been become a reality.

There have been other stories. A decade ago I attempted to describe what happened when sugar became an important item of European diet [Mintz 1985]. Unlike the potato, however, sugar was a luxury food that gradually worked its way down the European class ladders, starting as a plaything of royalty and becoming a necessity of working people only much later. Its generous use in hot, strong tea marked the first time a working class anywhere became deeply dependent upon foods—in this case, produced mostly by mass coercion—shipped to them from the ends of the earth. Power was quite visible in the story of how all of this had happened.

In that instance it seemed to me that power could be conceptualized in two strikingly different ways. The first and more obvious expression had to do with who produced sugar, seized the needed land, assembled the necessary machinery and labor (at the outset and for a very long time, enslaved labor), saw to shipping and marketing the product, and so on. But the other, less obvious form of power had to do with what consuming sugar came to *mean*. As a rare and costly substance, its very consumption expressed a kind of power—much as our consumption of costly caviar or fresh abalone or fine wine does so, today. The king's ability to display and consume sugar was one of the ways for defining his power. Over time, as the production of sugar rose, its price fell and its consumers multiplied. There was no longer any need for the power of the king to be signaled by the foods he consumed. Such power now inhered in the commercial ascendancy of the state, its colonial dominions, its power to tax, the benefits of the trade it oversaw, protected, and benefited from.

But for those millions who had not eaten sugar before, or had lacked the means to offer it to their loved ones or guests in various forms, the earlier and older sense of power in consumption could hang on. Not surprisingly, it does still, in every towering wedding cake, St. Valentine's Day candy box, and favorite dessert. The American G.I. in World War II with his chocolate bars embodied a modern rendering of that centuries-old form of power. For most Americans, the high point of the meal is the dessert, and even very good restaurants in this country show deference to our renowned sweet tooth.

For many people, eating particular foods serves not only as a fulfilling experience, but also as a liberating one—an added way of making some kind of a declaration. Consumption, then, is at the same time a form of self-identification and of communication. The employment of food to achieve a feeling of well-being or freedom is widely felt and understood. Much of the symbolic overloading of food rests particularly in its utility for this purpose. The satisfactions seem modest; the meal one eats in confirming that "you deserve a break today" may be neither expensive nor unusual. And yet this act of choosing to consume apparently can provide a temporary, even if mostly spurious, sense of choice, of self, and thereby of freedom.

The idea of *choosing* to consume lay behind giving this book its title. The essays themselves, of which the book is composed, were written at different times and for different purposes. But they all deal with the ways that human beings eat, investing their acts and the substances they consume with their history, their hopes, and their persons.

In chapter 2, I try to explain how the exercise of power affects what gets consumed, and under what conditions. In this instance, war is the background constant against which people—both soldiers and nonsoldiers—are enabled to stay alive. In doing so, they become identified with the foods they learn to eat. The core question this poses is: how do we apprehend or come to know foods (including here processed foods and brands, such as cheeses, soft drinks, breakfast cereals, salted dry "munchies," ice cream), then turn them, conceptually as well as physically, into parts of ourselves? By what means do those who make and sell us what we consume affect our symbol-making so that their products "become us"?

In chapter 3, I take up a special instance of the right to eat, in which the background constant is enslavement. The use of cooking by slaves as a means to escape the definition of themselves imposed on them by others is a case of tasting freedom.

In chapter 4, I attempt to show how the history of food is not simply one of successive changes unfolding through time, but something more. The triumph of sugar, the product of extraction, over honey, the product of living insects, is an unfamiliar chapter in the history of foods, and is documented here.

The next two essays explore other meanings of sweetness. In chapter 5, tasting freedom takes another form. Orwell's language, in which slavery *is* freedom, may be relevant. The sweet taste seems to awaken moral sentiments, at least in Western societies.[2] Because sweet foods are thought to be particularly fattening (as well as particularly tempting) in the United States, their place in the thinking of people intent upon losing weight can be much exaggerated, and the moral worth of self-restraint may come to turn on the dessert course. In this chapter, the moral or ethical positioning of sugar in modern society is assessed. Freedom for some people means becoming what one wants to be; dieting and exercise are thereby changed into the keys to a certain kind of freedom. I mean to raise questions here about the possibility of a morality so individualized as to make relatively little reference to society, except in the ways that the individuals themselves construct. How do self-fulfillment and social fulfillment fit together?

Chapter 6, "Color, Taste, and Purity" is a historical essay about a special sweet product, marzipan, which evolved from the combination of almond paste, sugar, and other ingredients. The whiteness of almonds and sugar is viewed here as part of their secret: whiteness is seen as equalling purity. Such an equation apparently has a special history in the West.

Chapter 7 is concerned with how one defines cuisine. Like the previous chapters, it is concerned with eating and with how human beings view eating. Who has a cuisine? How can we tell? This is not so obvious as it may seem; I try here to explain why. Having a lot of different ethnic foods to eat is not the same as having a cuisine; eating out a lot is not the same as having a cuisine. What does it take to have a cuisine? And does it matter?

The final chapter is a kind of extension of the discussion of cuisine: an attempt to talk about how we Americans eat. It is not a "scientific" essay—mostly a look at American food habits from the perch of one American. But I try here to take up once more the link between food and power, in reflecting upon where the U.S. food system may be going, during the next generation or so.

Many of these essays, as I have already indicated, were taken out of a body of work carried out over a number of years, and selected as the most relevant or useful in a collection of this sort. My hope is that they will make people think more about what they eat and why they eat it: about this amazing, everyday activity by which we stay alive. I am myself regularly astonished by what seems to me to be the un-self-reflective manner in which so many Americans eat what they do, under the conditions they do. I wish from time to time that they would do otherwise. My reasons for thinking that way are merely a personal legacy from my father. Eating can be—should be—one of our greatest joys, I think. For fifteen-year-olds, it usually is; but lots of people who are older than that somehow manage to lose their joy in eating, and never even know how and why it happened, usually attributing it simply to aging. If eating is anything less than joyous for you, I hope you'll think about why. And if by some special circumstance this book helps you to revise or rethink your opinion, then I shall not have written in vain.

chapter two
FOOD AND ITS RELATIONSHIP
TO CONCEPTS OF POWER

How does a society learn to consume food differently: to eat more food (or less), to eat different food, differently prepared, in different contexts; to revise or modify the social (and perhaps even the nutritive) purpose of the consumption itself? This chapter has two aims. I want to block out the kinds of constraint that can define the situations where people accept the necessity of changing their food habits. Then I want to illustrate how, having changed their food habits, people try to cope with the changes in their own ways by creating new consumption situations, endowed with new meanings which they themselves have engineered.

The use and application of power frequently enter into changes in a society's food consumption habits. Where this power originates; how it is applied and to what ends; and in what manner people undertake to deal with it, are all part of what happens when food habits change. We do not understand these processes at all well, even though they are of immense importance to the world's future. Nor do I believe that much of the research on changing food habits addresses the cultural aspects of such changes. I think that group values and past practices can figure significantly in what changes, how much and how fast. Thus culinary history enters into the success and failure of new applications of power in the sphere of food and eating, but not in readily understood or carefully studied ways. I attempt here to explain, though only in a preliminary fashion, my own ideas of how power serves to advance (or retard) changes in food habits.

SUGAR, TEA, AND THE BRITISH WORKING CLASS

In my book *Sweetness and Power* [1985], I contended that the heightened use of tea, sugar, tobacco, and a few other substances which came to typify the spending habits of the eighteenth-century British working class probably provide us with the first instance in history of the *mass* consumption of imported food staples. The hope in that book was to be able to explain the peculiar attraction these novelties had for new consumers. But the argument remained incomplete in part because I found it impossible to locate and isolate some specific single cause for this new consumption. Many explanations had turned up in the literature; none seemed to me particularly convincing. Two historians, sniffing the air anew, have recently settled on "the quest for respectability" as *the* cause [Austen and Smith 1990; Smith 1992, 1995]. Respectability, concrete and specific as it sounds, takes us part of the way, by building on the path-breaking work of Norbert Elias.[1] Yet we still do not really know why so many English people so rapidly became such eager consumers of sugar and tea, for example. The term "respectability" can be an umbrella for such things as hospitality, generosity, propriety, sobriety, social rivalry, and much else. The unanswered (and perhaps unanswerable) question persists, if what we aim at explaining is the peculiar power of a *specific* food (or even some category of foods) over consciousness and will. I earlier noted that possible factors influencing the British adoption of sugar included: the powerful stimulant contained in tea and other new beverages, coffee and chocolate, with which sugar was consumed; the common malnutrition of the British working classes at the time, such that the caloric contribution of sugar would matter unconsciously as well as consciously; the apparently universal predisposition of the human species toward the sweet taste; the readiness of people in most (if not all) societies to emulate their "superiors" if permitted; the possible significance of the element of novelty; and the usefulness of tobacco and the stimulant beverages in easing the industrial work day [Mintz 1985]. Faced with such a list, it becomes harder to talk about the relationship between some specific food and the exercise of power in society.

The emergence of British sugar-eating and tea-drinking took place against a background of overseas expansion and colonial conquest, which brought about a mounting commerce in enslaved Africans, and a growing number of plantations in the colonies. At home British society was undergoing increasing industrialization, the dislodgment of rural populations, and urbanization. Sugar, earlier a rare and precious imported medicine and spice, became at this time cheaper (at first rapidly, then more gradually); and while its cost went down, the uses to which it could be put proliferated. Sugar's increasing availability facilitated the increase in contexts within which it was used.

Once sugar began to be consumed by those of modest income, its employment for new uses increased swiftly. It entered into the rhythms of daily life particularly in its association with three new stimulant beverages: chocolate, coffee, and tea (in Brit-

ain, tea soon emerged as most successful). Much later and by a series of successive steps, sugar became important in its own right
—that is to say, other than in association with these beverages.

Meaning

In studying materials dealing with home and work conditions in
Britain in relation to sugar and other substances, I found it useful
in 1985 to separate the broad changes in background that made
access to sugar easier, on the one hand, from the circumstances of
daily domestic life and work, within which consumers installed
sugar in their everyday routines, on the other. On this basis I pro-
posed two terms to simplify discussion. The daily life conditions
of consumption have to do with what I called *inside* meaning; the
environing economic, social, and political (even military) conditions with *outside* meaning.

Inside meaning arises when the changes connected with *outside* meaning are already under way. These grand changes ultimately set the outer boundaries for determining hours of work,
places of work, mealtimes, buying power, child care, spacing of
leisure, and the arrangement of time in relation to the expenditure of human energy. In spite of their significance for everyday
life, they originate outside that sphere and on a wholly different
level of social action. In consequence of these changes, however,
individuals, families, and social groups must busily integrate
what are newly acquired behaviors into daily or weekly practice,
thereby turning the unfamiliar into the familiar, imparting additional meaning to the material world, employing and creating
significance at the most humble levels. This is what happened to
tea-drinking, once people tasted tea and were learning to drink
it regularly; and what happened to pipe-smoking, once tobacco
had been tried and was liked. People alter the micro-conditions
as much as they can and according to their emerging preferences
—the where, when, how, with whom, with what, and why—

thereby changing what the things in question signify, what they *mean* to the users. New behaviors are superimposed upon older behaviors; some behavioral features are retained, others forgone. New patterns replace older ones.

This happens, however, within the widest constraints that *outside* meaning allows for. I have just suggested that the processes that endow behavior with *inside* meaning unfold in relation to what I label "grand changes." But of course for the participants the micro-conditions themselves are, or become, grand—for it is out of them that the routines of daily life are fashioned. This interior embedding of significance in the activity of daily life, with its specific associations (including affective associations) for the actors, is what anthropologists often have particularly in mind, I think, when they talk about meaning in culture.

Some of us tend to be inordinately moved by the power of our species to invest life with meaning on this intimate, immediate, and homely level. Of course it is essential to stress the remarkable—even distinctive—capacity of our species to construct, and act in terms of, symbols. But in the case of the large, complex societies with which we deal today, it is at least as important to thorough understanding to keep in mind that larger institutional subsystems usually *set the terms* against which these meanings in culture are silhouetted. In daily practice, for example, job opportunities tell people when they can eat and how long they can take to do it; to a noticeable extent they also therefore tell people *what* they can eat, where, and with whom. Individuals are thus presented with a series of situations within which they may begin to make meaningful constructions for themselves, as long as such constructions do not violate the outer situational boundaries that have been established for them. But the job opportunities are determined by forces that transcend the means and wills of those who become the employees—as anyone who has lost a job recently knows.

In contrast to *inside* meaning, it is those larger forces expressed in particular subsystems, together with the state, that have to do with what I mean by the term *outside* meaning. Thus, *outside* meaning refers to the wider social significance of those changes effectuated by institutions and groups whose reach and power transcend both individuals and local communities: those who staff and manage larger economic and political institutions and who make them operate.

In the case of the history of sugar in Britain, these larger institutions were the servants of the imperial political and economic system, who carved out the West Indian colonies and gave them governments; who saw to the successful—immense and centuries-long—importation of enslaved Africans to the islands; who bequeathed land wrested from the indigenes to the first settlers; who financed and managed the ever-rising importation of tropical goods to Britain, including chocolate, coffee, cotton, and tobacco, as well as sugar, rum, molasses, tea, and much else; and who levied taxes at all levels of society, to benefit its servants and the state. It will soon become clear that these background arrangements of conditions against which *inside* meaning can take on its characteristic shape—what I call *outside* meaning—are cognate with what Eric Wolf [1990, 586–87] has labeled "structural power."

Using the word "meaning," rather than "power," in the first of my labels (*outside meaning*) may have been somewhat misleading, but there was a reason for it at the time. During recent years many anthropologists have been abandoning an older interest in how things are caused—no longer trying to explain why *this* happened, rather than *that*—in order to interpret events in terms of what they were supposed to mean. Such a shift in emphasis is thought to have brought the fieldworker into view, to have humanized anthropology while demystifying both the fieldworker and the fieldwork situation.

Yet this stress on meaning has also led us away from seeking to explain what happens (or happened) over time. We know that particular events often *mean* different things to different persons or groups in the same society. The slave trade and slavery "meant" that the British factory and farm workers would get their sugar; but the meaning of slavery and the slave trade to plantation owners, bankers, and the Colonial Office was entirely different. (One need hardly add that, for the slaves and their descendants, it also "meant" quite different things.) Anthropologists who are still interested in how things happen and the consequences of events, more than in what things may mean, need to be able to distinguish among different meanings, and different sorts of meaning, in order to continue to study causes and causation.

The abstract system we call "a culture," and the abstract system of meaning that is thought to typify the members of the society who "share" that culture, are neither simple coefficients of each other; nor two sides of one coin; nor merely the active and passive aspects of one system. To treat them as if they were is to bypass the complex nature of any society, and to impute to its members a homogeneity of value and intentions they almost certainly lack. *Outside meaning* is a term invented to avoid the imputation of any such homogeneity.

As for *inside meaning*, the use of "meaning" is entirely appropriate here, I think. Those who create such *inside* meaning do so by imparting significance to their own acts and the acts of those around them, in the fashion in which human beings have been giving their behavior social significance as long as they have been human. The gradual emergence of a food pattern called "high tea" among working-class Britons, for instance, was the work of those who eventually came to take this meal regularly; it was they who created the pattern. But they did so inside the constraints of work and income and their own available energy, constraints over which they themselves had hardly any control at all.

The connection between outside and inside meaning can be exemplified with a more modern case than that of sugar and tea in eighteenth-century Britain. But before looking at this case, we need to take note of a general paradox having to do with the whole issue of food and food preferences. On the one hand, food preferences, once established, are usually deeply resistant to change. We cannot easily imagine the Chinese people giving up rice to eat white bread, or the Russian people, black bread to eat maize. Such deeply cherished tastes are rooted in underlying economic and social conditions, and they are surely far more than simply nutritive. But they must also be viewed in terms of the equally telling fact that *some* preferences, even in diet, turn out in fact to be quite readily surrendered. To be sure, it is far more common to add new foods to one's diet than it is to forgo old and familiar ones. The readiness of the North Americans to become eaters of *sushi*, which surely could not have been predicted in 1941—and not only for political reasons—is an apt example of an unexpected, even unpredictable adding-on. Somewhat more interesting in the present argument is the gradual decline in the consumption of complex carbohydrates by North Americans over the past seventy-five years, which has meant not just the addition of new foods, but also a palpable decline in the consumption of certain once-prized old ones. But in any event, these addings-on and gradual eliminations are often hard to explain, for they proceed against a substantial, persisting stability of diet at the same time.

We do not understand at all well why it can be claimed both that people cling tenaciously to familiar old foods, yet readily replace some of them with others. Hence situations of rapid change in food habits deserve a much closer look than they have received. We need to know far better than we do now why some food habits change easily and swiftly, while others are remarkably enduring. We are inclined to view this contrast as between basic or essential foods on the one hand, and less important or peripheral foods on the other. But this is not adequate to explain all particular cases of rapid change. When much else is changing, food habits may change, too, and such changes are often unpredictable. Where and how power comes to permeate these processes of change, projected in part against continuing stability, is not always apparent.

A CASE

Here, then, is one example of how power enters into the changes that affect food choices; but it is a large-scale and general case. It has to do with war. War is probably the single most powerful instrument of dietary change in human experience. In time of war, both civilians and soldiers are regimented—in modern times, more even than before. There can occur at the same time terrible disorganization and (some would say) terrible organization. Food resources are mobilized, along with other sorts of resources. Large numbers of persons are assembled to do things together—ultimately, to kill together. While learning how, they must eat together. Armies travel on their stomachs; generals—and now economists and nutritionists—decide what to put in them. They must do so while depending upon the national economy and those who run it to supply them with what they prescribe or, rather, they prescribe what they are told they can rely upon having. During World War II, upwards of fifteen million Americans were brought together in uniform, many millions more in mufti. The service people ate together, in large camps. They ate what they were given; what they were given was decided by powerholders who functioned outside the army and outside their direct experience.

Among other things, service personnel were given meat twenty-one times a week; even the Friday dinner had an alternate meat course (though it was usually cold cuts). For most soldiers (but only irregularly under combat conditions), never before had so much meat been thrust before them. They were also given vast quantities of coffee and of sweets of all sorts; there were sugar bowls on every table, and twice a day, without fail, the meal ended with dessert. (As it happens, soldiers were also given free cigarettes while standing in line for their paychecks each month.) Though the food habits of the civilians may not have been altered so radically, certain things did happen, about which much is known. They got too little meat; and the wartime media were full of stories and jokes about romancing the butcher. They got too little sugar, too little coffee, and too little tobacco. Their food habits, too, were being radically affected. Hence North American food preferences—though "preferences" is more than a little misleading, under the circumstances—were significantly re-shaped by the war experience.

Among the things that soldiers and civilians were *not* given was Coca Cola; but careful arrangements were made to allow them to buy it. George Catlett Marshall, chief of staff during World War II, was a Southerner. It was soon after Pearl Harbor that General Marshall advised all of his commanders and general officers to request the building of additional Coca Cola bottling plants in order to get the product to the front. By his letter Marshall gave Coca Cola the same status in the wartime economy as that occupied by food and munitions. Coca Cola was thus spared sugar rationing. In all, sixty-four Coca Cola plants were established in allied theaters of war, including the Pacific theater, North Africa, Australia, and elsewhere. The Coca Cola Company was asked by the armed forces to supply technicians to run the production; 148 bottling plant technicians were sent; three were even killed in theaters of war during World War II [Louis and Yazijian 1980].

In the light of Coca Cola's status by the time the war ended, it is noteworthy that, before the war, Coke was not a truly international drink—I would claim it was not yet even a really national drink.[2] Though Coke had traveled early in its career to Cuba, it was still principally a U.S. beverage, mainly consumed in the South. There were foreign countries where it was sold, but it was not yet well known internationally. I suspect that its most numerous consumers in the U.S. were high school students who laced their Coke with Southern Comfort whiskey so that they could get publicly (yet covertly) intoxicated at the senior prom. Indeed, it is probable that most people outside the South didn't drink Coke, but "mixed" it instead. During the war, the fact that the United States professional officer corps was largely Southern may have played a role in this story, as well.

How *outside* meaning influenced the spread of Coca Cola is easy to discern. The rapid proliferation of Coca Cola bottling plants in allied theaters of war had much to do with its growing popularity. Power over labor and resources employed in the production of food undergirded the unhampered operation of the corporate system, closely coordinated in this instance with the will of the state. Even in times of politico-military crisis—some might say particularly in such times—corporate power neatly integrated with the state bureaucracy firmly underwrites the successful execution of what are defined as broader societal tasks. At such moments, the power of the state itself seems far less irksome to corporate America. The deployment of resources for food production is linked to conceptions of consumer choice as well. But in this instance the choices were managed in a specific fashion: 95 percent of all soft drinks sold on American bases during the war were products of the Coca Cola Company. There was choice; but one company only was accorded the right to specify its limits.

In contrast to *outside* meaning, *inside* meaning in a case of this kind has to do with what foods come to mean to those who consume them. The symbolism connected with Coca Cola, as it took on its national stature during the war, and as documented by such writers as Louis and Yazijian [1980, 50–67] and Pendergrast [1993, 199–217], was utterly astonishing. It may be relevant that soldiers overseas have not only been stripped of almost all of the marks of their individuality (clothing, jewelry, coiffure), but because they are in a remote land, they also feel bereft of those material representations of their culture that are embodied in architecture and in linguistic forms (familiar buildings, signs, advertising). Under such circumstances, which can be alienating, objects that can "carry" a displaced sense of culture, such as foods and beverages, take on additional potential power. Coca Cola turned out to be a nearly perfect symbolic repository. It was not unusual to find in the letters that servicemen wrote home the assertion that they were fighting for the right to drink Coca Cola. The *inside* meaning of Coca Cola is certainly revealed in the emotions of a soldier who fights—among other things—"as much to help keep the custom of drinking Cokes as I am to help preserve the millions of other benefits our country blesses its citizens with"—to quote from one of many such references to Coke in the censored mail of wartime. Thus it was that Coca Cola was enabled to become a symbol—a veritable national symbol—among the warrior youth of the 1940s generation.

War, then, is a setting in which the exercise of the power behind *outside* meaning readily applies. Such examples do not have to do with the intrinsic nutritive significance of food. They help to explain, rather, how outside processes serve to impose many of the conditions within which *inside* meaning can take shape and manifest itself.

CONCLUSIONS

In his lecture to the American Anthropological Association annual meetings some years ago, Eric Wolf [1990] enumerated four sorts of power. By Wolf's reckoning there is, first of all, personal power, of a sort comparable to *charisma*. Second, there is the power of persuasion, by means of which one person exacts conformance of some kind from another. Third, and on a broader canvas, there is the "power that controls the settings in which people may show forth their potentialities and interact with others" [p. 586]. This "tactical or organizational power" is "useful for understanding how 'operating units' circumscribe the actions of others within determinate settings." Tactical power can be used, for example, by organized business entities, such as multinational corporations, banks, and conglomerates. The exercise of such power is tightly linked to the background social conditions which affect food habits. But even more important is Wolf's last category. He writes of:

> a fourth mode of power, power that not only operates within settings or domains but that also organizes and orchestrates the settings themselves, and that specifies the distribution and direction of energy flows. I think that this is the kind of power that Marx addressed in speaking about the power of capital to harness and allocate labor power. . . . I want to use it as power that structures the political economy. I will refer to this kind of power as structural power. This term rephrases the older notion of "the social relations of production," and is intended to emphasize power to deploy and allocate social labor. These governing relations do not come into view when you think of power primarily in interactional terms. Structural power shapes the field of action so as to render some kinds of behavior possible, while making others less possible or impossible. [pp. 586–87]

When this perspective is applied to the subject of food habits, it is easy to see how structural and tactical (or organizational) power aligns the institutional frameworks that set the terms by which people get food, maintain or change their eating habits, and either perpetuate their eating arrangements and the associated meanings, or build new systems, with new meanings, into those arrangements.

All living organisms are faced with an imperious necessity: not to eat is to die. But beyond this, foods have meanings that transcend their nutritive role. Just as our species seems always to have made food carry symbolic loads far heavier than those of simple nutrition, so, too, the symbolism seems ready to spill over into even wider fields of meaning. The place of rice in Japanese culture, of bread in the West, of maize to many Native American peoples—these significations clearly surmount any literal nutritive significance the foods themselves might have.

It might seem acceptable to say, then, that food exercises "power" over people in terms of what it means to them. But that is *not* the sort of "power" with which I am dealing; and it is important to be clear in this regard. The material world is invested with meaning. Because people act in terms of understood meanings, meaning can be said to effectuate behaviors of certain kinds. And power and meaning are always connected. "Power is ... never external to signification," Wolf writes. Power "inhabits meaning and is its champion in stabilization and defense" [Wolf 1990, 593]. But the symbolic power of foods, like the symbolic power of dress or coiffure, is different from (even if related in some manner to) the tactical and structural power that sets the outermost terms for the creation of meaning. The power resting within *outside* meaning sets terms for the creation of *inside*, or symbolic, meaning.

Turn again to the words of that earnest GI who fought to preserve his right to drink Coke. There is no question about *inside* meaning in this instance. Such *inside* meaning is linked to *outside* meaning because what Coke means is coefficient with its history as a commodity, with the steps taken to ensure its availability, with the history of those very decisions by which Coke could become the purchased soft drink, the tie to home, the exciter of nostalgia, a very symbol of America. What I call *outside* meaning and *inside* meaning are clearly linked in Coke's story. But they are also quite different from each other, and they do not stand in any simple relationship.

In his own work, Wolf has set apart the issue of meaning from the issue of power. But he sees them as inextricably connected. He writes: "Meanings are not imprinted into things by nature; they are developed and imposed by human beings. Several things follow from this. The ability to bestow meanings—to 'name' things, acts and ideas—is a source of power" [Wolf 1982, 388]. As this essay attempts to suggest, the ability to "supply" things, in the broadest sense, is also a vital source of power, not only because it may include some ability to bestow meaning, but also because meaning coalesces around certain relationships. Objects, ideas, and persons take on a patterned structural unity in the creation of ritual, as happened, for example, when "high tea" became a working-class eating custom. But it was the purveyors of the foods, the givers of employment, the servants of the state who exercised the power that made the foods available.

If we return briefly to the case of sugar in eighteenth-century Britain, we may inquire of the material to what extent the creators of background conditions can be said to set the precise terms for the emergence of *inside* meaning. Emulation, for example, played some role in increasing and in shaping food use; so, probably, did medical advice. The conditions under which landless people worked were determined by others: the hours when they might eat or rest, where they took their food, how they got to and from work. At the level of daily life, the customary practices that working people developed in order to deal with the newly emerging industrial society in which they found themselves were answers, or "solutions," to conditions over which they had no real control. In these ways, *outside* and *inside* meanings are linked through the conditions created and presented to potential consumers by those who supply what is to be consumed.

This chapter has aimed at clarifying these questions. But what is needed is a concerted effort to study the various ways in which stable food habits can be called into question. We may also ask ourselves *why* they are called into question. Some answers may have to do with poor nutrition, overeating, or inordinately expensive cuisine, relative to available resources. But other answers may have little or nothing to do with health or economy, even though people are being subjected to intense pressures to forgo some parts of their diet in favor of different foods. At times, as has been suggested here, large-scale structural changes, such as war and migration, may change the rules of the game, so to speak, compelling people to reorder their categories of meaning in new ways, and to eat (and drink) differently. How this is done, and why it succeeds, urgently need to be understood. So, too, do all the means used to persuade people that what they are eating now should be replaced with something else. I think that it is within anthropology's capabilities to confront these issues solidly; but so far it has not done so. Until anthropologists try to find answers to these questions they will not be able to contribute in full measure what they can to our understanding of the world food problem.

TASTING FOOD, TASTING FREEDOM

To understand the meanings of food in slave consciousness in Caribbean societies, one needs to examine the slaves' lives, and the lives of their descendants, on a level of detail that may capture the imagination of neither scholar nor reader. Yet such detail is significant. I believe that the homely, everyday experiences of the slaves bore importantly, if indirectly, upon bigger issues—perhaps even on the abolition of slavery itself, and the eventual realization of freedom in different epochs and countries.

The crowning achievement of the struggle to end slavery was freedom itself. But freedom of what, and freedom for what? The enslaved knew what it was to be free, before they were enslaved; they were captives who could remember freedom.[1] Their children, born into slavery, may have known about "being free" as their parents told them of it. But they also knew of "freedom" as defined by the colonial societies in which they lived; the free people in those societies were almost as different from each other in their rights and fates as were former slaves and present masters. Being free, in other words, was not some single homogeneous status, even if one never mistook it for slavery.

In the obvious and most important ways, what the slaves wanted in wanting to be free is dreadfully clear. But freedom could mean other things besides freedom from cruelty, sexual aggression, and exhausting labor, imposed by the will and sadism of the master class. It could mean being free to move about, to marry, to choose one's work. It also could mean freedom to choose one's friends, one's clothing, and yes—even one's food.

The distinguished Andeanist John V. Murra once suggested that we conceptualize exploitation as the denial to individuals or groups of customary prerogatives of the human condition as defined by the culture [see Mintz 1961b, 87]. In some such broad framework for the denial of equal rights, New World slavery from 1503 to 1888 would represent a wide range of variation. It was a system that allowed some things to the slaves. But what it denied varied from decision-making and freedom of movement in vitally important spheres of life down to many small details. The hardship that it imposed on people must have been experienced as varying from gross and hideous injustice—as in the case of branding, rape, flogging, or the forced separation of family members—to an endless series of petty annoyances, irritations, and quixotic but inescapable afflictions.

Seen from this perspective, I believe that the taste of freedom and the taste of food may be much more closely linked than they seem at first to be. The taste of freedom sounds so empyrean, noble (or ennobling); the taste of food, so ordinary, so material. But these "tastes" are not really so remote from each other. It is possible to suggest ways in which these seemingly quite different perceptions may be linked. In doing so, I seek to bring together things that belong together conceptually but that have drifted—or have been kept—apart.

Why one would look at food and freedom together is not mysterious. We are told often, and insistently, that man does not live by bread alone. I think most of us know that already. But we also know that man (and for that matter, woman) without bread cannot live at all. This platitude appeals less to the not-by-bread-alone folks than their own platitude. Still, a shortage of bread—even as it excites useful reflection on who profits from the unjust distribution of bread—may provoke a glorious nobility of thought. In seeking, then, to join stomach to mind, I do not mean to violate a natural separation; I claim that it is the separation which is unnatural.

It was the great British anthropologist, Audrey Richards, who pointed out in *Hunger and Work in a Savage Tribe* [1932, 1] that the need to eat is the most basic need we human beings know, far exceeding in importance and urgency the sexual "drive." We know that people usually have strong feelings about food—about what they eat and what they don't eat. We also know that people are enculturated to eat just about anything, including numerous toxic substances—as well as to claim that whatever they eat is the best or only good food for real human beings. We are currently much aware that people use food and eating socially for lots of different purposes—to send messages, for example, about their status, gender, and group membership. But the stress in this chapter will be as much on foods—their origins, their modes of production, their processing, and their preparation—as on their meanings.

In the Caribbean region in the slavery era, capture and transportation of Africans were followed by the terrible test of plantation toil, experiences which seriously disturbed those parts of the ancestral cultures which could be "carried" by the enslaved. They had to reconstitute their ways of life under daunting conditions, in new and unfamiliar settings, and in the absence of the full institutional structure of their societies of origin [Mintz and Price 1992].

Given the central importance of food in the lives of all peoples, it is not surprising that what the slaves got to eat, what they could produce or catch to eat, and how they came to create a cuisine of their own became building-block features of slave culture. The origins of such foods may seem to be the least telling part of the story. But diversity of origins provides an important lesson in the construction of culture—a lesson that Afro-Americans had to learn probably more fully than any other people of modern times.

Tasting freedom is another matter. The argument here will be that the slaves not only had taste and canons of taste, but also that their taste in food influenced the tastes of the masters. Many of the foods the masters would come to eat and prize in so-called slave societies they would learn about from the slaves. Those who caught or grew the food, who prepared and cooked it, who contributed most of all to the creation of the cuisine, were the slaves themselves.

The masters enjoyed freedom, wealth, leisure, and a near-total monopoly of power. In contrast, the slaves were cruelly overworked, frequently malnourished, and ill. Since the food provided to them, if at all, was usually shameful in quantity and quality, it is not surprising that they were often accused of theft, and no doubt they often did "steal" food.[2] But of course it was their labor that produced local wealth; and it was they who *created* Caribbean cuisine.

The core importance of slavery for Caribbean societies was in the provision of masses of labor power at low cost. But once it was installed as a system, slavery developed—as social institutions do—its own rationale. By employing slaves other than for brute labor, the slave system recognized their humanity; it was thus that the master class itself dramatized and institutionalized the central contradiction of slavery. In the act of creating a cuisine the slaves exercised human skills at a substantial remove from the initial economic objectives of the slave society. For those purposes the slaves came to enjoy an unanticipated freedom of maneuver.[3] It was not equally available to all slaves—to those whose tasks were to feed and manage animals, plant cane, collect fodder. Yet nearly all of the slaves had something to do with food, with its production or processing or distribution. In these differing tasks (and in eating), they were able to exercise the human potentiality to taste, to compare, to elaborate their preferences. To be sure, they did so under terrible constraints; often, just staying alive was the sole challenge. Yet the ability to render judgments of food, to develop comparisons, to calibrate differences in taste—and to be prevented from doing so—help to suggest that something of the taste of freedom was around before freedom itself was. The tasting of freedom was linked to the tasting of food. I will try here to suggest how.

Caribbean slavery began around 1503 and ended in 1886. Its life span, then, was almost four centuries. It involved half a dozen European powers (as well as the United States and Brazil). During the course of the trade, it is conservatively estimated that about nine and one-half million enslaved Africans reached the Americas [Curtin 1969, 87]. Nearly a third—about 2.6 million—reached the Caribbean islands [Mintz 1971b, 438]. In other words, a tiny geographical portion of the Americas absorbed an immense number of enslaved people, during an epoch that stretched over four-fifths of post-Columbian history. So unusual a demographic concentration was a consequence of the development of the plantation economy.

These enslaved peoples were consigned principally to agricultural labor in the Caribbean region, particularly on plantations and especially sugar plantations—large-scale agricultural estates producing basic commodities for European markets, including coffee, tobacco, chocolate, indigo, cotton, and, above all, sugar, rum, and molasses. The first enslaved Africans brought to Santo Domingo in 1503–1505 worked on sugar plantations, and the last enslaved Africans smuggled into Cuba in the 1860s or 1870s worked on sugar plantations—a depressingly enduring continuity.

In spite of the near-industrial character of the plantation, the slaves did create for themselves distinctive ways of life, drawing on their own traditions, and on what the new settings offered them. These new cultures are usually described in somewhat misleading fashion as "mixed" or "blended." They are, in fact, *sui generis*—neither African nor European, but Afro-American. Their accurate characterization must take many different factors into account, to escape from literal, mechanical, two-plus-two or coffee-and-cream analogies. Even a brief look at the development by enslaved Africans of a distinctive Caribbean cuisine reveals the variety of factors to be considered. For convenience, I have divided the following discussion into five topics: (1) the origins of foods; (2) the production of foods; (3) the processing of foods; (4) the distribution of foods; and (5) the emergence of cuisine.

THE ORIGINS OF FOODS

The foods of the slaves came from all over the world. Some, such as cassava (*Manihot esculenta*), maize (*Zea mays*) and peanuts (groundnuts) (*Arachis hypogaea*), were aboriginal New World cultigens, which (as it happened) diffused to Africa and became parts of some African cuisines, thereupon returning, Africanized, to the New World. Names for these three plants or for foods prepared from them (such as Haitian Creole *bambouri* for cassava cakes, Jamaican Creole *pindar* for peanuts, and Haitian Creole *akasan* for cornmeal porridge) attest to lexical adaptation; hundreds of food words in the New World are African, and many (like these) are for American foods. Once in Africa, such foods became African in much the same ways that potatoes became Irish, and tomatoes Italian. Other plants were native but minor Caribbean cultigens that became known and used by the slaves, such as the tuber *Calathea allouia* (Spanish *llerén* or *lirén* from the Taíno name, Haitian and Trinidadian Creole *topinambou*, Dominican *topitambour*), the capsicums or "hot" peppers (for example, *C. frutescens* or *C. annuum*), and the spice *Bixa orellana* (called *annatto* in Jamaica, *achiote* in Puerto Rico, and *roukou* in Dominica). Salted dried codfish and herrings were imported from Canada; their importation paralleled the growth of slavery in the region. Some foods imported by Europeans originated elsewhere, such as swine and eggplants. Some came from the American mainland, including papaya (*Carica papaya*) and, later, potatoes and tomatoes (though by way of Europe, it appears). Arrowroot (*Maranta arundinacea*) was present on only some Caribbean islands and diffused elsewhere in the Antilles after Columbus. African cultigens included coffee, one species of rice (*Oryza glaberrima*), and melons. Okra (*Hibiscus esculenta*), which came from Africa, was originally Asian; all its American names are African. Other foods that were originally Asian included taro (*Colocasia esculenta*, commonly called cocoyam in West Africa), mangoes (*Mango indifera*), and breadfruit (*Artocarpus altilis*). In some cases we have specific records of diffusion. For instance, it seems that the banana (*Musa acuminata*) reached the New World in 1516 from the Canary Islands, carried by a friar, Padre Berlanga. Captain Bligh, commissioned by the Jamaica Assembly to bring the breadfruit (*Artocarpus altilis*) from Oceania, was successful on his second attempt, and was feted in 1794 for his achievement.[4] Other plants and animals came from Africa, possibly carried by the slaves themselves. Among them, I suspect, was the yam with an aerial bulbil, *Dioscorea bulbifera*, which the Haitians call *masòkò*, the Bambara and Mandingo name for another yam species. Probably some herbs, both medicinal and for food flavoring, also arrived in this fashion.

Thus the origins of Caribbean foods are enormously wide, representing in large measure the origins of Caribbean peoples themselves: Africa, Asia, the Middle East, Europe, and the New World. But the first Africans arrived enslaved. Mere survival must have absorbed their energy for some time after they arrived. The food they got was given to them. The conditions of survival, and the resources available to be built upon, were mostly new and strange. Hence to fashion a cuisine was a great accomplishment, and it happened not once, but repeatedly. In effect the slaves had arrived in a world they then had to remake for themselves.

The origins of particular crops and food items may seem to matter little in the total picture of slavery. Yet it mattered much in regard to the way that new cuisines were built up over time. In this as in much else, a kind of *bricolage*—a French word for "patching together" made famous by the great French anthropologist Claude Lévi-Strauss—occurred. The slaves quickly displayed their readiness and ability to draw freely upon what was available in recreating with new content and in new form their own distinctive cultures.

It makes too little of cultural creativity to call this creation of a new cuisine a "mixing" or "blending" of culture. One might as well reduce the Afro-American development of jazz to a "mixture" of borrowed and traditional sounds. *Creativity* always involves *change*. Slave cooks did far more than put historically unrelated foods into the same pot; by creating new dishes they made familiar foods taste different.

THE PRODUCTION OF FOODS

Most plantation slaves suffered because the labor demanded of them was intense and exhausting, the level of treatment extremely harsh. Often they had to live—at times, barely—on the rations supplied to them by the estate. Barry W. Higman [1984], writing about the British Caribbean, 1807–1834, notes three principal food sources: imports, estate production, and garden production by individual slaves.[5] Imports included such foods as salt cod and cornmeal. But this was a costly—and risky—solution to the need for slave food. In the British Caribbean, food imports declined sharply after 1807. Estate production of food

tasting food, tasting freedom

—in which slave gangs were supervised while they produced their own subsistence collectively—was never important in the smaller British islands and lost its importance early in most such colonies. The chief handicap here was in taking the slaves away from the main task of producing plantation exports.

Hence it was the slaves themselves who commonly emerged as the major food producers, working in family groups and on their own time, producing the bulk of the food of free people and their own as well. In Jamaica, to pick an example, in the early nineteenth century the plantation slaves produced most of the food on plantation uplands: sweet potatoes, cassava, maize, taro, plantains, *malanga* (a term used for two different edible rhizomes, both the New World *Xanthosoma sagittifolium* and the Asian-African *Colocasia esculenta*), pigeon peas, vegetables, herbs, even rice. Certain minor items were grown near the slave huts; the bulk of the food was grown at some distance, on poor hilly land not used for the plantation crops. This distinction between "yard" and *polink* (Jamaica) or *lakou* and *jadin* (Haiti) has persisted up to the present in Caribbean life. Of the cultivation practices we know little. But we do know that family groups worked the land; that the choice of crops was in the hands of the slaves (though the masters sometimes complained); that the masters commonly respected the slaves' claims (for instance, in usufruct); and that the slaves eventually were producing most of their own food.

It became stylish at one point to speak of this development as a "breach in the mode of production" [Lepkowski 1968, Cardoso 1987], and the interpretation of such proto-peasant production as a form of active resistance has now become pronounced.[6] But that the provision plots were an extraordinary by-product of New World slavery has been recognized for a very long time.[7] Created at the insistence of the masters to reduce the cost of feeding slaves, the plots and then the markets were to become training grounds for freedom, a basis for the eventual rise of a free peasantry [Mintz 1971b, Besson 1984, Trouillot 1988]. I have dubbed the slave cultivators of their own food supplies "proto-peasants"—still enslaved, they engaged in productive activities on their own time, to their own (as well as their masters') benefit, developing the skills they could use, once free [Mintz 1961b].

THE PROCESSING OF FOODS

Food processing includes everything that must be done to foods between harvesting (or capture) and cooking—winnowing, grinding, sifting, washing, peeling, grating, straining, and so on. It also involves changing the composition of the food to make it edible or more appetizing. A good example is the processing of manioc, which contains a deadly poison, and the preparation of which entails a lengthy and labor-intensive detoxification.[8] Fish and game must be scaled or skinned, gutted, and often boned; peas must be shelled; coffee dried, decorticated, washed, and roasted; maize stripped from the cob.

Such processing is linked to knowledge of the nature of particular foods (and, thereby, to taste), and the organization of plates, courses, meals, and cuisine. The connections between floral and faunal knowledge, food and culinary knowledge, are often intimate. In Caribbean societies such as Haiti and Jamaica, for instance, eaters of yams (*Dioscorea* spp.) in the countryside often can describe different species and varieties of yam; they may include in their descriptions not only yam size, shape, and color, but also texture, "dryness" or "wetness," "sweetness," and taste.[9] Such knowledge is not new. By the start of the eighteenth century, at least six yam cultivars were being produced on slave plots in Jamaica, for instance. Yams were an important food in many of the African societies from which the ancestors of those proto-peasants came, but plant and taste taxonomies had to be restructured in the new settings.

Much as with the slaves' production of food, its processing

was also linked to the assignment of tasks and the division of labor, both on the plantation and within the slave family. There are tasks needing more strength or less, one person or several. These "simple" problems in the division of labor are anything but simple—as anyone knows who has tried to put up a roof, caulk a canoe, or prepare a six-course dinner for ten persons. Both production and processing posed logistical problems for the slaves, and the solutions they devised required that dependents—children, the elderly, the retarded, the impaired—all play important roles. Organizing production and processing of food meant that the slave family gained autonomy despite the plantation structure and was an arena of socialization in which childhood and parenthood took on what are, for us, familiar meanings.

There are some clues to this in the literature. William Beckford, for instance, writing in 1790 of the proto-peasants of Jamaica, observes that the tasks of cultivation are familial:

> Upon these occasions they move, with all their family, into the place of cultivation; the children of different ages are loaded with baskets, which are burdened in proportion to their strength and age; and it is pleasing to observe under what considerable weights they will bear themselves up, without either murmur or fatigue [1790, 2: 440–44].

In the plantation gang, socialization of this sort simply could not have occurred.

THE DISTRIBUTION OF FOODS

The single most important development in the distribution of Caribbean foods during slavery was of internal market systems. Once little studied, these systems, like the slave provision grounds, are now receiving unprecedented attention. Over time such systems were forms both of resistance and—though less noticed—of accommodation by the slaves, steps on the path from slavery to freedom. In the Saint Domingue and Jamaican markets of the late eighteenth century, one could find European vegetables, African rhizomes, and New World starches and fruits, in addition to fish and shellfish, Guinea hens and pigeons, goats and swine [Mintz and Hall 1960]. There is no more eloquent witness than Moreau de St. Méry, writing of the marketplace of Clugny in Saint Domingue, in the years preceding the Revolution, where 15,000 slaves would congregate each Sunday to buy and sell their own products [1797, 1: 440–44]. The markets enabled the slaves to produce what they (or the markets to which they sold) desired and thus influenced both the breadth and the stability of cuisine.[10] The markets made both slave cultivators and slave cooks familiar with a wide range of foods—creating demand and stimulating supply at the same time. We do not know whether slave cooks traded recipes or shopped themselves at local markets for the produce they would use. We know that the foods in the use of which they became expert were local and predominantly produced by slave cultivators.

THE EMERGENCE OF CUISINE

The specific foods mentioned earlier all eventually figured in the emergence of cuisines, but of course not all at once.[11] The introduction of plants, foods, recipes, and cooking methods depended to some extent on the succession of movements of peoples to the region. European and African dishes, cooking methods, and specific foods figured most importantly in the evolving cuisine, but American cultigens such as cassava, maize, and sweet potatoes were persistently important. African bananas/plantains, Asian taro, breadfruit, and mangoes, and European vegetables entered early into cooking practices and are examples in the substantial repertory of foods. Local fish, turtles, mushrooms, birds, and herbs also found their place; the slaves played a cardinal role in installing such foods in local life.[12]

The most important features of Caribbean cooking originated in the popular diet of local people. Though without Africa it is difficult to imagine what Caribbean cuisines would be like, the same could be said of Europe and the New World, not to mention Asia. Each Caribbean cuisine represents an unusually creative synthesis of plants, foods, dishes, and cooking methods from all over. We cannot escape the theoretical problems posed for us by the processes of synthesis and interpenetration— of foods, of ideas, of peoples.[13]

Cuisine itself is an important part of the story, but it is also difficult to discuss historically. We have seen that the slaves were poorly provided, often half starved. Despite the many laws prescribing cultivation or rations, slaves commonly died of hunger, and a prime reason for *marronnage*—running away—was hunger. In Jamaica before emancipation, rats were a common article of commerce. It is essential to remember these facts to avoid giving the impression that the slaves ate whatever they liked, or that they often ate well. Yet it is important to stress the culinary part of life as one in which a special sort of autonomy was nonetheless exercised.

"Cuisine" as used here refers to three different things. First, it means what the slaves learned to eat upon their arrival; that food was usually cooked by other slaves, and some of it was familiar. Commonly it was a complex carbohydrate, such as maize, prepared as a porridge, eaten with greens, and extremely meager quantities of animal protein, such as salt cod or beef. Barry Higman [1984] suggests that planters often thought more about the food for children than for adults, and there were sometimes extra rations for sick slave infants. Breakfasts were often cooked for the slaves and served at work: boiled yams, mashed plantains (Puerto Rico: *mofongo*), sweet potatoes, breadfruit boiled in soup or roasted, together with boiled salt cod, were among the dishes.

Pepperpots and broths served to extend protein. Molasses was seasonally provided in some regions. Of this part of the cuisine nothing general can be said in regard to quantities, other than that most slaves in most places were undoubtedly undernourished.

The second use of "cuisine" refers to what the slaves cooked for themselves. Though we skate on thin ice factually, it seems likely that at first the foods tended to be the same as those served to the slaves by the plantation. Yet we know that slaves who earned money through market activities used their earnings to buy delicacies, or to improve the quality or quantity of their food intake; while slaves who cultivated could stabilize food uses that were otherwise impractical. They fished, gathered, and trapped, as well as farmed. Archeology has provided rich clues about diet,[14] and a few descriptions refer to the slaves at their meals.

Finally, "cuisine" refers to what slave cooks cooked for the masters and their families. This picture is utterly different; almost any diary or travel book of the time gives some indication of the food. For instance, Lady Nugent's diary provides a number of fairly detailed descriptions of meals taken in Jamaica in the early period from 1801 to 1815 [Cundall 1939, 93, 95, 121 *passim*]. Imported foods were expensive; many European staples could not be easily shipped abroad. Slaves had to employ local and seasonal items, including a large variety of crustaceans, fish, and wild fowl. Creole poultry and meats, especially pork and goat, but also chicken and duck, and rarely beef, were eaten. Turtle and manatee and semiferal swine were often used, as well as a staggering variety of starchy foods, both cereals and rhizomes, and vegetables and fruits from all over. The use of spices was more substantial than in Europe. Jamaica, for instance, produces the indigenous pimento or allspice (*Pimenta officinalis*) used in cooking fowl, in pickling, and to make a flavored liqueur. The capsicums (peppers), also New World in origin, were present throughout the Antilles and entered into the emerging cuisine. Imported spices such as nutmeg (and its arillode, mace), ginger,

coriander, and turmeric did well in the region, and were important cuisine ingredients. Papaya leaves were used to soften meat
and fowl, annatto to color (and flavor) rice, arrowroot starch to
make gravies, and so on. Slave families coped always with poverty of resources, including fuel; the basic cuisine is fuel-
economical. Yet the high value that came to be put upon rice
and—though less important—the need to eat much boiled
starchy food and the tougher cuts of meat runs counter to the
principle of fuel economy.

The cooks in planter families had the opportunity to eat best
and to cook with the best equipment and food repertory. One
wishes we knew more of their lives, how they were trained, how
they might innovate, and how they saw themselves in relation to
the other slaves. That they played a special role both in stabiliz-
ing cuisine and in diffusing it more widely through their cooking
outside the great house seems certain.

CONCLUSIONS

I have stressed that before emancipation the cuisine of slaves was
marked by monotony and poverty of resources. Under such circumstances, to claim that the cuisine was a slave-created system
and that the tastes of food and of freedom were linked may seem
exaggerated. But it would be easier to believe that it was an ex-
aggeration if the difference between submission and resistance
were crystal clear—and it isn't. Dealing in food was dealing in
freedom at many levels. For example, working in the production
of food legitimized certain claims that the slaves would level
against their masters; working in the distribution of food legitimized freedom of movement, commercial maneuver, association,
and accumulation; working in the processing of food legitimized
the perfection of skills that would become more important with
freedom; and working in the emergence of cuisine legitimized
status distinctions within slavery, both because the master class

became dependent upon its cooks, and because the cooks actually invented a cuisine that the masters could vaunt, but could not themselves duplicate.

I think that there were two quite different, but equally important, forms of oppression that operated on slaves in the Caribbean and made more difficult the emergence of a solid Afro-American culture. First there was the obvious pressure of terribly hard work, accompanied by the constant threat and exercise of violence—all of the hideous difficulties for people created by enslavement, transportation, and continuing abuse. But there was also another, second pressure, at least as destructive as the first, and with different consequences; this was the living ideology of slavery as practiced and preached by the masters, and what it signified. An ideology of justification, it commonly involved assumptions about African cultures and the alleged innate incapacities of Africans and their descendants to function autonomously in a society controlled by Europeans. To the extent that the slaves could be successfully described as incapable of surviving independently, in the eyes of the planters the system justified itself. This, perhaps, is the point. Because of the inherent contradictions in treating human beings as if they were not human, as animal chattels, the ideological space between what the slaves *were* and what the ideology *said* that they were, was repeatedly enlarged by the activities of the slaves themselves. Each time, it became an arena for another sort of struggle: one in which the human propensities of the slaves challenged the explicit assumptions of the planters.

I have deliberately picked a humdrum aspect of daily life in order to argue that our understandings of the slaves' experiences must be integral understandings—we must try to understand how the slaves coped as whole persons with their condition. Their behavior shows that indeed we do not live by bread alone, but that our hearts and our heads are intimately connected to our stomachs. Eating is not merely a biological activity, but a vibrantly cultural activity as well. Under slavery, this activity, like all else in slave life, had to be rebuilt and endowed anew with structure and meaning, by the slaves themselves. Slavery shredded the whole of the material life of its victims, penetrating the very cell of the family, tearing people loose from their cultures, lands, and kin groups. But in the New World the slaves remade their lives culturally. They drew upon their ultimate resources as human beings, and they succeeded by struggle in keeping their humanity intact. They did so, as human beings have always done, by giving meaning to their own achievements.

THE CONQUEST OF HONEY BY SUCROSE: A PSYCHOTECHNICAL ACHIEVEMENT

INTRODUCTION

In this chapter I want to look at the differences between the world's most ancient sweetener, honey, and what is today the most used of all sweeteners, sucrose—the pure white granular substance we call "sugar." The contrast between these substances can be exemplified by noting modern attitudes toward honey and sucrose in the United States. But it can also be posed for those centuries when, in Britain, honey and sucrose were first brought into contention for what were in most ways the same markets. Cane sugar did not simply replace honey as a primary sweetener. The way the struggle was waged provides us with an early example of how what is called "consumer preference" works itself out in practice.

The unfolding histories of honey, cane sugar, beet sugar, maple sugar, high-fructose corn syrup, and the noncaloric sweeteners reveal at once the divergent interests of sweetener producers on the one hand, and the persistent sweet tooth of humankind on the other. During the seventeenth and eighteenth centuries, Europeans in large numbers learned for the first time to consume substantial quantities of cane sugar, while the consumption of honey remained modest, and probably even contracted. Though much else has of course happened since that time to change the world sweetener picture, the rivalry between cane sugar and honey persisted during a century or more, preceding cane sugar's resounding victory. It is with that contest that the present chapter is principally concerned.

CONTEMPORARY ATTITUDES IN THE UNITED STATES

Honey and sugar pose an important contrast in contemporary life. In popular thought, sugar is "solid" (crystalline), honey "liquid" (syrupy); sugar is "pure white," honey "golden"; sugar is "refined" (chemically pure), and honey is "natural" (hence, "naturally pure"). Thoughtful persons will have remarked that sugar has "no taste"—by which is meant that its sweetness is neutral, so it may be freely mixed with coffee, chocolate, vanilla, or individual fruit flavors, for instance, without changing their distinctive tastes (while also implying that each of these other substances has some single, integral, and readily recognizable flavor). In contrast, honey is perceived quite correctly as having a distinctive "taste" (or, more accurately, *many* distinctive tastes), which are imparted to any substance that is combined with any honey. Moreover, in the United States—and doubtless in other places as well—honey is viewed as somehow more traditional, more "authentic" (whatever that means: Americans might say "more homey"), and—as already noted—more natural, than sugar. Though the differences between sucrose and honey with regard to such health matters as tooth decay and nutrition are at most slight, honey is also commonly regarded as more nourishing or more healthful.

Such perception in regard to these two foods merely suggests what is already well known in regard to popular opinions generally: that they are approximations of objective reality and reveal folk conceptions of that reality. Moreover, we know that such opinions may persist, relatively undisturbed, even in the face of apparent contradictions or unexplained inconsistencies. But as is almost always the case, such opinions are also often not entirely off the mark, and may touch unexpectedly upon historical, sociological, and natural-historical facts. Thus, for instance, everyone associates honey with bees. When asked, people may state that honey is both "collected by" and "made by" bees. At the same time, most persons seem to think that sugar is "manufactured" from something (rather than freed in a liquid medium from plants). When taken together, these views, neither entirely false nor entirely true, are surely one source of the interesting belief that *therefore* sugar is "less natural" than honey. And while a great many people are astounded to learn that sugar has not "always" been part of Western diet, most also seem to assume—correctly—that honey has been with us for much longer than sugar, even if they are unprepared to make any guesses about the relative antiquity of these substances as foods.

It is in the sphere of so-called "naturalness" that the contrast between sucrose and honey seems most spectacular today, at least in the United States. Interest in the "naturalness" of foods has appeared to rise and fall in this country by a series of odd oscillations. The last such big increase in interest in "natural" foods— by no means abated—seems to have coincided with the anti–Vietnam War protest movement, one of a complex of concerns about military adventurism, war, the draft, conservation and environmental pollution, vivisection, political corruption, and involvement in numerous other public interest issues (as well as in "exotic" philosophies and religions). In seeking personal answers to social problems, whose causes were imputed to an irrational scientism, to corrupt political leadership, and to a deep disregard for Mother Nature, many young North Americans turned toward religiously prescribed diets, different degrees of vegetarianism, special cooking devices and arrangements, fresh fruit and vegetable juices, high-fiber cereals, and other "natural" foods. Honey was conspicuous among them.

In this unfolding scenario, sucrose did not do well, though various means were found in the United States to enhance its marketability, even under relatively unfavorable conditions: artificially "coarsened" brown sugars; the use of brown sugars in "natural" cereals; the (usually unadvertised) combination of sucrose with what are perceived as "healthier" and "more natural" foods, such as yogurt, berries, and nuts (for example, "yogurt-covered almonds"); the substitution of technical terms for various sugars (such as writing "sucrose" instead of "sugar," or writing "less sugar" while adding more dextrose) on package descriptions of contents; and—more recently—campaigns that more aggressively extol sugar's low-calorie content as compared with that of many other foods and its own "naturalness" when compared with artificial sweeteners. Sugar producers in the United States have been particularly exercised over the trade name "Nutrasweet" for aspartame, claiming (on good grounds) that sucrose, unlike Nutrasweet, actually provides nutrition. (The comment that aspartame is "only a chemical" has not been equally convincing as a pro-sucrose argument. However, at least some journalists writing for laymen seem to be attracted by that view, even arguing on the basis of little data that artificial sweeteners may, by their eventual effects, actually *increase* caloric intake.) At the same time that some sugar companies have been vying with the drug companies manufacturing artificial sweeteners, of course, they have also struggled with the currently privileged position of high-fructose corn syrups within the highly protected domestic market for sugars, and have done so in part by buying into that production.

Historical Background

Competition among different sweeteners is an old story. Hence it may be instructive to turn back in history to the appearance of sucrose in relatively large quantities in Europe for the first time, and to spell out something about its emerging relationship to honey, since the potential consumer territory these foods then occupied was contested.

Honey is, of course, much the older sweetener for our species, and there is no doubt that it has been prized by at least some human beings for millennia. As a product that could be gathered from wild hives, its use may very well be coeval with the emergence of our species; and the behavior of many nonprimate mammals certainly supports the likelihood that pre-*sapiens* hominids also sought and avidly ate honey [Dams 1978, Crane 1983]. As the principal source of intense sweetness for humankind until the mastery of the crystallization of sucrose, honey has carried an immense symbolic, mythic, and psychological load. This has been conditioned in part by the somewhat mysterious nature of its production, "... a by-product of the survival of plant-species by insect pollination" [Crane 1976, 3]. In literature and in myth, honey has been the food of the gods, the symbol of the Promised Land, the sweetest poetic symbol in literature, and an important source of sexual metaphor. Though the time came when sucrose shared some of the burdens of meaning, in Europe this would not be until the start of the present millennium.

Of sugar, there is little need to say here more than that crystalline sucrose was certainly known in the Far and Middle East by the early centuries of the Christian Era, and perhaps earlier.

the conquest of honey by sucrose

Greek visitors to India *may* have become familiar with sucrose (*saccharon*) there, as well, at the outset of the Christian Era [Forbes 1966, Mintz 1985]. By the thirteenth century, sucrose was reaching England in modest quantities, where it was first used principally as a spice, or medicinally. Its price, N. Deerr believes, remained consistently higher than that of honey during the fifteenth and most of the sixteenth centuries [1949–50, 2:528]. But for various reasons—among them the abolition of the monasteries under Henry VIII in 1537, and the consequent decline in demand for candle wax! [Crane 1976, 475]—honey production contracted in the sixteenth and seventeenth centuries, while the supply of granular sugar and molasses rose. Thereafter there appear to have been fairly steady declines in the price of sugars, such that sugar eventually became a much better buy for equal sweetening. In all likelihood there has been no time since at least 1800 when the price of honey and the price of sugar have approached each other again, save perhaps in wartime.

HONEY AND SUGAR AS SPICES AND BEVERAGE BASES

Sugar—sucrose—won out over honey as an item of *mass consumption* in the eighteenth century and has never retreated. The product it bested had never bulked importantly in medieval diet. European pre-sucrose sweet foods included the characteristic fruits of temperate Europe—apples, pears, cherries, and berries, for example—and honey. But honey was not so common as might be supposed, nor was it eaten in large quantities. Finally, it was not an important article of trade. Eva Crane thinks that the reason honey figured so rarely in the accounts of large households in the Middle Ages is because most kept their own bees [1980, 115]. She supposes that average annual per capita honey consumption in medieval Britain may have been no more than perhaps two kilograms, and adds:

It is commonly said that honey was then "the only sweet-ener" for most people, but sweetness was not at all a com-mon characteristic of foods. The present high consump-tion of sweet foods and drinks in many countries is a concomitant of the growth of the sugar industry, and has little to do with honey. [118]

This persuasive observation brings into view two issues: the place of sweetness in European cuisine at the time that sucrose was still a rare and expensive luxury; and more generally, the uses to which honey was put, in pre-sucrose Europe.

As to the first, I have stressed elsewhere that the use of honey in cooking—and of sucrose, as it became available—ought not really to be called a "sweetener use," so much as a "spice use." Recipes from the *Forme of Cury*, the fourteenth-century cook-book of the chefs of Richard II, suggest that honey—and by that time, sugar as well—figured frequently in the diet of the noble and wealthy, even though not in the diet of the poor [Warner 1791]. Yet the quantities were really small. "It used to be thought," writes M. W. Labarge [1965, 96] "that sugar was unknown until later in the Middle Ages, and that only honey was employed for sweetening; but a close study of accounts shows that sugar was in continuous use in wealthy households by the middle of the thir-teenth century." The quantities employed, however, even in the kitchens of the wealthy, suggest that "sweetening" may be the wrong word. The Countess of Leicester's household accounts for a seven-month period in 1265, for instance, reveal that fifty-five pounds of sugar (of two sorts) were purchased for her kitchen in that period; yet the purchases of pepper (presumably *Piper ni-grum*, or Indian peppercorns) for the same period amounted to fifty-three pounds [Labarge 1965]. Spices, almost invariably in tiny quantities and mixed with other flavors, typified the fare of the rich [Sass 1981]. The "basic spices" were pepper, ginger, saffron, cinnamon, and cloves, but sugar was used frequently as well [Laurioux 1985, 66]. In England in the fifteenth century, Laurioux tells us, sugar is found in 40 to 50 percent of the recipes. Galingale (a relative of ginger), saffron, saunders (powdered sandalwood), mace, cardamom, and other spices were eventually employed as well to flavor food; sugar in equally modest quantities was added with them. Though inexact, the recipes of the time do make clear that the relative quantities of spices and sugar were similar, and sparse:

> Take chykenns and boile hem in gode broth, and ramme him up [bruised, and pressed close together]. Thenne take zolkes of ayren [eggs], and the broth, and alye [mix] it togedre. Do thereto powdor of gynger, and sugar ynowh [enough], safronn and salt; and set it over the fyre withoute boyllynge, and serve the chykens hole, other ybroken [or cut up], and laye the sowe [sauce] onoward.
> [Warner 1791, pt. 1:9]

There seems little doubt that, in recipes of this sort, sugar *is* a spice. "The reason for the immoderate use of spices," writes W. E. Mead [1967, 77]:

> may be found in part in the current opinions on diet in the Middle Ages. Most men knew that the enormous amount of meat served for a feast, or even for an ordinary meal, imposed a heavy burden upon the digestion, and hence they used cinnamon and cardamon and ginger and many other spices to whip up the action of the stomach. Even when not at table they made free use of spiced comfits, partly for the sake of aiding digestion and partly to gratify the appetite. One may well believe, too, that at a time when overkept meats and fish were freely used, spice was employed to cover up the incipient decay. At all events, whatever the reason, most dishes were smothered

in spices, whether needed or not. As a rule, possibly because of its provenance from the East, sugar was classed
with spices.

Cooks were certainly aware that honey and sugar do not really
taste alike. Some recipes called for both. But except for particular
baked-goods recipes in which honey is a principal ingredient,
most recipes between the thirteenth and nineteenth centuries not
only suggest a steady increase in the number of sweet dishes in
common use, but also a steady replacement of honey by sugar.

Honey was used in two other particularly important ways: as
a basis for alcoholic drinks and medicinally. Though the origins
of its use as a beverage base are shrouded in antiquity, fermented
honey drinks are mentioned in the Bible and in Indian epics.
D. E. Le Sage has studied the terminology of honey and mead in
Indo-European languages. He concludes that "the very small
number of separate roots behind the various Indo-European
words for honey is remarkable indeed," and continues:

> With the special exception of Germanic, only two pri-
> maeval honey terms provide all the Indo-European lan-
> guages with their attested terminology: *melit-* and
> *medhu-*. [The linguistic use of the asterisk indicates a re-
> constructed word; the hyphen, that it is a word stem.]
> *Medhu-* occurs in virtually all Indo-European lan-
> guages, and in one (eastern) section its descendants de-
> note both "honey" and "mead" (or other alcoholic drink)
> without distinction, whereas in the other (western) sec-
> tion *medhu-* means mead only, and honey is denoted by
> a derivation of *melit-*. [1980, 428]

Le Sage's findings attest to the ancient and wide diffusion of the
use of honey as an intoxicant beverage base, and as late as the seventeenth century, honey-based fermented drinks remained important in Britain. Honey was fermented with water or another

liquid to make mead, or to be mixed with, for example, wine, grape juice, or rose water to create what would now be regarded as somewhat exotic, honey-based intoxicants (including metheglin or hydromel).

However, as the importation of both wines and sucrose rose during the last quarter of the seventeenth century, when British Caribbean sugar production was also rapidly increasing, candied and spiced wines such as hippocras became more popular with the British upper classes. The English "put a great deal of sugar in their drink," P. Hentzner [1757] wrote in 1598; and when Fynes Moryson discussed English drinking habits in 1617, he commented:

> Clownes and vulger men only use large drinking of *Beere* or *Ale* . . . but Gentlemen *garrawse* onely in Wine, with whiche many mixe sugar—which I never observed in any other place or kingdom to be used for that purpose. And because the taste of the English is thus delighted with sweetness, the wines in tavernes (for I speak not of Merchants or Gentlemens cellars) are commonly mixed at the filling thereof, to make them pleasant. [Rye 1865, 190]

Just as sugar began to replace honey in its "spice" use, so it seemed to have done the same in regard to intoxicating beverages. Added to this was the transformation of molasses—in effect, a by-product of the extraction of sucrose from cane—into rum. The sturdy official support provided sugar producers, when the state made mandatory the issuance of rum to H. M. Navy personnel, also deserves notice. In 1698, only 207 gallons of rum were imported to England; in the period from 1771 to 1775, however, annual average importation had risen to well over 2,000,000 gallons. The Navy ration began unofficially after the capture of Jamaica in 1655; it became an official daily half-pint from 1731 on and was increased to a pint per day for adult sailors toward the end of the eighteenth century.[1] Thus both as granular solid "spice" and as a source of a liquid intoxicant, sugar made its assault upon honey. But quite possibly even more important than either of these usages was the employment of molasses (or "treacle," as it came to be called) as a food and beverage sweetener. To explain that use of molasses, however, it will be useful to look first at the medicinal usages for honey and sugar.

H ONEY AND SUGAR AS MEDICINES AND SWEETENERS

European medical practice of the seventeenth century, when sugar was first becoming plentiful and its price was beginning to fall, was deeply influenced by Galenic theory. The humoral medicine of Galen and Hippocrates, long cut off from Europe, had reentered European medical thought via the doctors and scientists of the Arab world, working in Toledo (Spain), Salernum (Italy), Gondeshapur (Khuzestan), and elsewhere. In all likelihood it was these scholars who added sugar in its various forms to Galenic usage, particularly for the mixing of medicines in a syrup medium. M. Levey explains that Arabic pharmacology was organized in terms of medical formularies, and "may be considered to have had its organizational origin in Galen's *De Compositione medicamentorum*; surprisingly, it persisted well into the nineteenth century as a form of pharmacological literature" [1973, 74]. Many of these formularies were of liquid medicines of varying viscosity. The syrup, for instance (Arabic *shurba*), was "a juice concentrated to a certain viscosity so that when two fingers were dipped into it, it behaved as a semi-solid when the fingers were opened. Very often sugar and/or honey were added as thickeners and sweeteners" [ibid]. Sucrose and honey were humorally distinguished, but both were considered "hot" by humoral scholars and were frequently used interchangeably. Seventeenth-century physicians such as Tobias Venner and James Hart described the medical properties of honey and sugar and compared their virtues and limitations [Venner 1620, Hart 1633]. Both were used for coughs, labored breathing, and sore throat, among other maladies, and to suspend other solid medicaments. This latter use is particularly instructive when we examine the origins of the English term "treacle," which first appeared in English with a medical meaning. Its origin is the Greek term for "of, or belonging to, a wild beast," and the "theriac" (or "treacle") was a compound medicine. The most powerful treacles usually included among their ingredients viper's flesh, since this was considered a specific for treating snakebites—hence the name. Treacles were suspended in a viscous solution, commonly honey. Over time, the liquid leavings of sugar manufacture, which the Americans call "molasses," came to replace honey in English medical usage. Since the medicines in which it was used were principally those where it could replace honey, either as a specific or as a semiliquid medium, the compounds themselves eventually lent their original name to the new syrup in which they were suspended. One F. Chance, in *Notes & Queries* for Feb. 27, 1762, writes:

> But how did our word, *treacle*, come to be *exclusively* used in so very different a sense, for the purpose, namely, of designating merely the "viscid, dark-brown, uncrystallisable syrup which drains from refined sugar in the sugar moulds" (Pereira)? I cannot say, unless it be that treacle very frequently enters into the composition of *electuaries* (or *confections*), and that so a name which was originally applied to a certain electuary only, ultimately, but in England alone, came to designate a substance, which, often forming the great bulk of electuaries, would naturally often resemble them both in appearance and consistence. [1762, 146]

Thus, in the case of medicine as in the cases of spice use and alcoholic beverages, the supplantation of honey by sucrose can be documented. There seems no doubt that these shifts in usage were impelled in part by the constantly increasing quantities of sucrose available, and the general decline over time in its price. But it seems likely that other features of the differences between honey and sucrose deserve mention, even though we cannot be certain of their importance in effecting the shift.

DIFFERENCES BETWEEN THE PRODUCTS

There are, to begin with, differences in degree of homogeneity. To be sure, the sugars of the seventeenth and eighteenth centuries were not standardized; both types and qualities (in the sense of chemical purity and degree of refinement) varied greatly. P. Pomet provides more than four pages of descriptive text on different sugars in his *A Complete History of Drugs* [1748], for instance. But the differences among sugars were reflections of technical limitations that could be gradually eliminated, so that attaining an extremely high degree of chemical purity was a finite and realistic goal for sugar technicians. Even those sugars described by Pomet were, in most cases, deliberate confections, fabricated to serve different purposes. Honey, on the other hand, varied enormously; it still does, and its variability both gives it its distinctiveness and ensures its lack of standardization.

Sugar was to become familiar to its early European consumers in both solid and liquid form. In its solid form, it varied from the less costly coarse, brown, imperfectly crystallized concretions called "loaves" or "heads," to the precious, quite fine, near-white loose granules or powder, then used principally for medical purposes. In its liquid form, as molasses (treacle), sugars also varied in purity, color, and viscosity. Treacle was less expensive than hard sugar; it became an important addition to puddings and pastries, and was at first used to sweeten tea as well. These two different forms of sugar heightened its versatility. Moreover, that one could "move up"—to use the U.S. advertising phrase—from cheaper and less pure forms to more expensive and purer forms may have positively affected the readiness of people to buy more sucrose. That sucrose began as a consumer good of the wealthy and powerful, only gradually percolating downward to become accessible to the poor, certainly had something to do with the eagerness with which its increasing availability was greeted. By contrast, honey was a local item, unimportant in trade, its production mostly individual and unorganized, appropriate to an era when foods traveled short distances only, and one-person technology sufficed for most productive tasks. Sugar, in contrast, had been an item of overseas production since its introduction into Europe, important in trade, its production highly organized and disciplined, appropriate to an era when mass-produced and mass-consumed foods had begun to travel vast distances, and gang production—for very long almost exclusively by enslaved labor—fitted the available technology.

Finally, it is worth mentioning the role of the organizers of production themselves in understanding more fully how sucrose conquered honey.[2] As the first imported luxury food to become a cheap daily necessity of the masses, sucrose epitomized the success of a rising industrial economy in tying the consumption of the workers to their increasing productivity. In the eighteenth century, to have all the sugar one wanted was to "eat like a king"—at least so far as sugar was concerned. But sugar—together with tea, tobacco, and alcohol—also turned out to be an eminently taxable commodity, and was duly transformed into a fiscal mainstay of the state. In this process, sugar acquired many champions in the press, in the medical journals, in the Foreign Office, and in Parliament.

It seems likely that advertising in the modern sense was born with products such as sugar, commodities whose production could be tied to the convenience of the colonies, to economies of scale, and to rising consumer buying power at home. Modern advertising is built upon the belief that increasing demand can be *created*, and that productivity will increase as perceived wants, expressed in demand, increase. Such ideas run counter to the mercantilist and utilitarian views of the past. Advocates of particular products had to struggle for a hearing, much as sugar had to struggle for a bigger piece of consumer buying power. Advertising helped, for it works by association—associating the product with what are otherwise desirable thoughts, admirable persons, divine causes, good health, good works. In the struggle to transform consumers familiar with honey into enthusiastic users of sugar, one chronicle may be worth the telling here, though it is merely exemplary.

At the Plaistow Wharf in London in 1883, Abram Lyle began making a refined molasses to which the name "Golden Syrup" was given. From a modest and relatively slow start, "Goldie," as it was called, eventually became the premier product of Tate & Lyle, with an immense and loyal clientele. "Abram III's strongly religious background," Anthony Hugill tells us:

> left its impression when it came to the difficult matter of choosing a trade mark, and an illustration from the story of Samson was selected. Hence the appearance on the can of the lion killed by Samson, and surrounded by bees, and the quotation from Judges XIV. "Out of the strong came forth sweetness (out of the eater came forth meat)." [1978, 53]

There is more to the story, however. The famous green-and-gold Golden Syrup tin shows a dead lion, the lion Samson killed, surrounded by bees; they have nested in the lion and made honey. Samson had asked the Philistines to answer his riddle: "Out of the eater came forth meat, and out of the strong came forth sweetness," but they didn't know the answer. It was Delilah who worried it from him and told the Philistines: "What is sweeter than honey? And what is stronger than a lion?" But of course Samson's riddle had to do with *honey*; Golden Syrup is made from *sugar*. Whether the motive of simple religious piety is convincing enough to account for the choice of a honey symbol to sell sugar syrup can be left to the reader to decide. It was a strategic choice in any event, epitomizing not only the besting of honey by its upstart but irresistible competitor, but also the birth of a new ethos for the honest description of one's products.

The triumph of sucrose depended on more than trademarks, however. Each instance of the replacement of one set of foods by another—the case of honey and sugar is only one of many—is complex and poses its own set of questions. But the meaning of the ousting of a local, small-scale industry by an international, large-scale industry is that it marked a fundamental change in the nature of European economic life. I have written elsewhere:

> The first sweetened cup of tea to be drunk by an English worker was a significant historical event, because it prefigured the transformation of an entire society, a total remaking of its economic and social basis. We must struggle to understand fully the consequences of this and kindred events, for upon them was erected an entirely different conception of the relationship between producers and consumers, of the meaning of work, of the definition of self, of the nature of things. What commodities are, and what commodities mean, would thereafter be forever different. And for that same reason, what persons are, and what being a person means, changed accordingly. In understanding the relationship between commodity and person, we unearth anew the history of ourselves. [Mintz 1985, 214]

Honey and sugar are useful to compare because each, in its way, stands for a different epoch in the history of human production. The details of their encounter need to be spelled out in a much more exacting fashion than I have attempted here. But perhaps this sketch of the background can suggest the usefulness of studying consumption "on the ground." Without the historical equivalent of ethnographic detail, our understanding of how new markets form and new products are enshrined in consumer preference scales will remain forever deficient.

chapter five
SUGAR AND MORALITY

From about the mid-seventeenth century onward, the consumption of sugar, at least in the West, appears to have been colored by moral judgments, both positive and negative. Much the same seems to be true now, as we stand on the brink of the twenty-first. In this chapter I want to speculate about why sugar and its use should have given rise to moral issues, and why they continue to do so.

In any society, at least some features of the act of eating will probably be encumbered with moral overtones.[1] The same for the act of not eating, when others eat. Each such act takes on its power as a vehicle for scoring moral points in contrast to the other: either of eating some things and not eating others; or of eating, or not eating, at all. To redefine the physiological act of ingestion as an arena for the classification and acting-out of moral principles is of course a distinctively human achievement. But it operates only according to rules that are culturally specific by their nature, not common to all members of the species. Here is one example.

In his only serious literary success, a personal memoir entitled *Father and Son*, the fin-de-siècle English critic Edmund Gosse calls attention in an arresting passage to the symbolic power of food, eaten and abjured. *Father and Son* is a remarkable work. Entangled within a biography of his father, it is Edmund Gosse's autobiography, from his first memories to the end of his youth. His father, the anti-Darwinian naturalist Philip Gosse, was a founding member of the Plymouth Brethren, an ascetic Calvinist sect. For Philip Gosse, food like everything else was a moral instrument. As the leader of a small band of the faithful, Philip Gosse decided on one occasion to bring a halt to backsliding among the parishioners by declaring without warning at the end of his sermon a one-day, bread-and-water fast of contrition: "Those of you who have to pursue your daily occupations will pursue them, but sustained only by the bread of affliction and by the water of affliction." To his son's amazement, the congregation apparently took this admonition wholly to heart. The nine-year-old Edmund was not excepted:

> How the rest of the congregation kept this fast I do not know. But it was a dreadful day for us. I was awakened in the pitch of night to go off with my Father to the Room, where a scanty gathering held a penitential prayer-meeting. We came home, as dawn was breaking, and in the process of time sat down to breakfast, which consisted—at that dismal hour—of slices of dry bread and a tumbler of cold water each. . . . We sat, in a state of depression not to be described, in the breakfast-room, reading books of a devotional character, with occasional wailing of some very doleful hymn. Our midday dinner

came at last; the meal was strictly confined, as before, to dry slices of the loaf and a tumbler of water.

The afternoon would have been spent as the morning was, and so my father spent it. But Miss Marks, seeing my white cheeks and the dark rings around my eyes, besought leave to take me for a walk. This was permitted with a pledge that I should be given no species of refreshment. Although I told Miss Marks, in the course of the walk, that I was feeling "so leer" (our Devonshire phrase for hungry), she dared not break her word. Our last meal was of the former character, and the day ended by our trapesing [traipsing] through the wet to another prayer-meeting, whence I returned in a state bordering on collapse and was put to bed without further nourishment. There was no hardship in all of this, I daresay, but it was certainly rigorous. My father took pains to see that what he said about the bread and water of affliction was carried out in the bosom of his own family, and by no one more unflinchingly than by himself. [Gosse 1907, 195–96]

Though eating is essential to continued life, both the use of food and intentional abstention from it are cultural practices revealed as the means of expression of powerful emotions. Such employments of food and fast are common enough to support a dependable cross-cultural assertion: the society that does not somehow use ingestion in this manner is rare, if indeed it can be shown to exist at all.[2]

Food habits can serve as vehicles of deep emotion. They are normally learned early and well and are mostly inculcated by affectively significant adults; hence they can acquire enduring sentimental power. One does not become an adult in the abstract; it must happen in terms of some particular, substantive body of cultural materials. Food and eating are positioned near the core of such materials because of their life-giving and essential (though usually routine and spuriously perfunctory) nature. As such, they are repetitively constitutive of one's culturally specific humanity. Children are trained accordingly. The learning of personal fastidiousness, manual dexterity, cooperation and sharing, restraint and reciprocity are commonly linked to the consumption of food by children. Indeed, getting to eat with the adults as an adult, rather than as a child, may be one of the major hurdles of growing up in some cultures.[3]

Perhaps moral conviction commonly attaches to this sphere of human activity because it is not only frequently practiced, regular, and necessary, but also because it is a sphere in which *some* choice is usually perceived as possible. For each individual eating is a basis for linking the world of things to the world of ideas through one's acts, and thus also a basis for relating oneself to the rest of the world. Food goes into every human being. Though it is not easy to explain or describe clearly, the intuition that one is somehow substantiated—incarnated—out of the food one ingests can be said to carry some kind of moral charge. It would probably be more surprising if, as symbol-using creatures, we did *not* burden ingestion, in one manner or another, with a moral onus. Among foods, however, processed sugar or sucrose is a latecomer with a somewhat special status.

A granular sucrose extracted in liquid form and processed from the sugarcane plant must now be about two thousand years old in the Middle East. Scarcely known in the West before the eighth century, sugar's introduction there dates mostly from the Crusades. After reaching Europe, and until it became a sweetener for more and more Europeans around the start of the eighteenth century, sugar was subject to powerful social, economic, and political forces which, among other things, changed it from a luxury and rarity into a prosaic necessity.

Yet throughout this time it remained a much-prized and affect-ridden treat, even if not always from the same class of consumers. Though at first used as a medicine and spice, sugar's distinctive taste became widely known in the West in association in particular with the bitter stimulant beverages, all of them exotic and novel in the seventeenth century: coffee, tea, and chocolate. Sugar also had an acquired association with tobacco, when chewed, and in some lands, including England, with alcoholic beverages, since it was often added to both.

Whether such associations noticeably affected the way sugar was perceived by its consumers, we do not certainly know.[4] We do know that the popularity of sugar in many western European countries continued to grow during the eighteenth and nineteenth centuries. Sugar consumption quintupled in the nineteenth century in the United Kingdom, even after having already risen at high rates for two centuries preceding. Northern Europe and much of middle Europe changed generally into heavy sugar-eating regions between 1750 and 1900, and the sugar-eating vogue spread outward, especially to major overseas anglophone areas (for example, the United States, Canada, Australia, New Zealand).

Questions about the suitability of sugar as food had been raised early in its history in the West. For example, Hart recognized in 1633 that "immoderate" use of sugar could rot the teeth [Hart 1633, Mintz 1985]. Other physicians questioned its usefulness in some treatments. But these were health issues, without a specifically moral dimension. Moral issues connected to sugar during its early history in the West did not have to do so much with sugar itself, as with related matters. Thus, for example, we find the moral place of sugar tested in relation to fasting. Thomas Aquinas found for it in this case. Aquinas was asked whether the eating of spiced sugars constituted a violation of the religious (Catholic) fast. He concluded that such sugars were medicines, not foods: "Though nutritious in themselves, sugared spices are nonetheless not eaten with the end in mind of nourishment, but rather for ease in digestion; accordingly, they do not break the fast any more than the taking of any other medicine."[5]

But another far more compelling linkage of sugar to morality marked events in the northern European country that had first proved itself most hospitable to it. In the early years of the final decade of the eighteenth century, British abolitionists who had hoped to abolish the slave trade came to realize they had lost that fight, at least for the moment. Parliamentary defeats of the special measures they had struggled to secure in 1791–92 led them to call for a new strategy. In effect, the decision was made to pursue the same goal, but this time through economic pressure rather than legislative action. In pamphlets and broadsides the abolitionists told their readers that the consumption of West Indian produce was tantamount to the commission of murder.[6]

As with all such political events, cartoonists found a funny side. In one cartoon dating from 1792, George III, his wife, and five unruly daughters are depicted (the royal couple had, in fact, only four), about to drink their sugarless tea. The daughters display varying degrees of disdain, while the anxious parents urge them to enjoy their refreshment. The Queen beseeches her daughters to drink bitter tea—"Consider how much work you'll save the poor blackamoors." The young ladies are unmoved.

But the abolitionists themselves were deadly serious about finding sugar eaters guilty for the sins of slavery. Lowell J. Ragatz [1928, 261] writes:

> Each user of Caribbean products was directly and personally responsible for the existing state of affairs. "Every person who habitually consumes one article of West Indian produce, raised by Slaves, *is guilty of the crime of murder*—every one who does it, when convinced that what has been said is true is *deliberately guilty*, and rendered more criminal by it being preceded by every species of cruelty and torture, which inventive barbarity and devise . . ."

The antisaccharites were imaginative:

> So necessarily connected are our consumption of the commodity, and the misery resulting from it, that in

every pound of sugar used (the product of the slaves imported from Africa) we may be considered as consuming two ounces of human blood. . . .[7]

All Christians were called upon to give a practical demonstration of the principles of their faith by refusing to use products defiled with blood; children were asked to forgo accustomed sweets and thus prevent the selling of their little black brothers into bondage; royalty was urged to set an example of abstinence which must needs be followed by all persons of importance in the country.[8]

The end of the trade in slaves came soon after the turn of the century; the end of slavery itself finally arrived, less than three decades later.

Boycotters and antiboycotters alike mixed morality and politics in their struggles. Sugar was not easy to forgo because it tasted so good. Those who gave up eating sugar because they believed their abstention would save lives were engaging in economic and political action of a moral kind, intended for the welfare of others.

Some critics of sugar, however, found the sugar itself to be morally questionable. In the anonymous *Essay on Tea, Sugar, Whitebread ... and Other Modern Luxuries* [1777, 13] (probably written by the reformer Jonas Hanway), the reader is first harangued about the evils of tea, and then:

To these we may add another pernicious Foreigner, called *Sugar,*—which not only inflames the poor man's expences, but his blood and vitals also. If you please, then, join them all together, and compute the expence, the loss of time taken in breaking and washing the dishes, sweetening the tea, spreading the bread and butter, the necessary pause which defamation and malicious

tea-table chat afford, and they will largely account for
half a day in winter, spent in doing that which is worse,
very much worse than doing nothing.

Hanway's tirades against tea and sugar criticize this use of
the laborer's income, the time wasted in consumption, and the effects of tea. Hanway does not criticize sugar so much; he even
concedes later that it may be beneficial in some ways. Yet his argument has moral implications: luxury and excess (sweets included) are corrosive of the will; wasting time and wealth are
both morally intolerable.

Though somewhat remote from these examples, another, different case bears mention here. In a provocative paper on the history of ice cream in Scotland, Francis McKee [n.d.] has documented the early inclination of Glaswegians to associate ice
cream with immorality, particularly (it seems) because the pio-
neers of ice cream retailing in Glasgow were Italians. McKee's
argument is provocative because the role of sugar (here, in the
form of ice cream) is given a sexual cast, in the manner of alcohol
and other substances that might be used for salacious ends. Thus
testimony before a Joint Parliamentary Committee is reported in
the *Glasgow Herald* of June 7, 1906, as follows:

> Cross examined, witness added that he had seen the
> boys and girls kissing and smoking and cuddling away
> at each other.... Detective Young, Northern Division,
> stated that he had known many little girls when about
> twelve or thirteen years of age who had since been before
> Magistrates, and were now prostitutes. The boys who
> had accompanied them as girls were now living off
> them, and were going out acting as their bullies at night.
> Q. Do you ask us to believe that the downfall of these
> women was due to ice-cream shops? A. I believe it is.
> [McKee, 1991, 7]

sugar and morality

McKee quotes A. J. Cronin's *Hatter's Castle*, which deals with that place and time:

> Now she was eating her macallum, a delicious concoction of ice-cream and raspberry juice, which, cunningly blending the subtly acid essence of the fruit with the cold mellow sweetness of the ice-cream, melted upon her tongue in an exquisite and unexpected delight. Under the table Denis pressed her foot gently with his, whilst his eyes followed her naive enjoyment with a lively satisfaction. [McKee, 1991, 8]

Again we see the association of sweet things with luxury and excess, and hence with issues of morality. Werner Sombart linked luxury to women in his treatise *Über den Luxus*, and sugar figures prominently in his list of luxuries:

> On one point, however, we already seem to have arrived at complete agreement: the connection between the consumption of sweets and feminine dominance....
>
> This connection between feminism (old style) and sugar has been of the greatest importance for the history of economic development. Because of the predominant role of women during early capitalism, sugar rapidly became a favorite food; and only because of the widespread use of sugar were such stimulants as cocoa, coffee and tea adopted so readily all over Europe. Trade in these four commodities and the production of cocoa, tea, coffee and sugar in the overseas colonies as well as the processing of cocoa and the refining of raw sugar in Europe are outstanding factors in the development of capitalism. [Sombart 1967 (1919), 99]

The links Sombart thinks he sees among women, luxury, capitalism, and a particular substance have robust moral coefficients.[9] In

the case of sugar, pleasure (of a morally dubious sort) can be con-
cretely located as originating in a specific substance.

McKee and Sombart descry a link between sugar and vice in
the first instance, sugar and excessive luxury in the second. As we
have seen, the abolitionists boycotted sugar in an effort to help
free the slaves. Here is another example of a religious boycott of
sugar—albeit not because of any intrinsic quality of the sugar
itself.

Redcliffe Salaman, author of *The History and Social Influence
of the Potato* [1949, 116] writes:

> When the Old Believers, following on Patriarch Ni-
> kon's reforms, broke away from the Russian Orthodox
> Church in 1667, the more powerful group of schismatics
> known as *Bozpopovschini*, or the "Priestless" [ones], re-
> garded certain foods and the like as abominations. Chief
> amongst these were sugar, tobacco and potatoes, none of
> which, it will be noted, are mentioned in the Bible. Cane-
> sugar, a luxury in England, must have been a great rarity
> in Russia of those days; tobacco and potatoes, both new
> arrivals, were not only rarities but, sharing the primal
> curse of the *Solanums*, were considered to be generated
> by some peculiar botanical form of incest.... Reverting
> to the fact that the three forbidden articles are not men-
> tioned in the Bible, it is noteworthy that many of the
> schismatics returned to a type of Judaism and added
> pork to their other taboos.[10]

The creation of a new taboo by a religious sect has many paral-
lels; it is of interest here only because one of the tabooed foods is
sugar. Collective repudiation of practically anything, whether it
be the practice of abortion or the words of a national anthem, can
figure importantly in the stimulation of positive in-group feelings, for those who share in the act ideationally. In the case Salaman describes, the *Bozpopovschini* were showing themselves to be

purer than the priestist (*popovets*) church they had abandoned because its priests and members had not renounced such foods. The
forswearing of foods (as well as the forswearing of particular taboos, as in the rise of Christianity) is a feature of religious change,
and seems always to be invested with moral weight.

The historical examples that have been provided up to this
point suggest that sugar has been foregone for the good of others,
as in the case of the antislavery antisaccharites; and for the sake of
God, as in the case of the *Bozpopovschini* and the Plymouth
Brethren. But what about repudiating sugar for one's own personal, moral reasons? Surely that sort of repudiation must figure
in any contemporary reflection on sugar and morality. Paul
Rozin has suggested three reasons why today's sugar-eaters may
consider sugar consumption morally dubious or sinful. First,
there is its association with "sinful" substances (such as coffee);
second, he posits an asceticism that views all pleasurable sensa-
tions as inherently questionable morally (a view that would over-
lap with the ideas of, say, Philip Gosse); and third, there is the
possible link between sugar and obesity, since obesity itself,
Rozin claims, can be perceived as sinful. [Rozin 1987]

That eating should be subject to such strong moral overtones
Rozin attributes to the intimacy of ingestion. I share this view.
But it needs noting that such association is highly variable cross-
culturally; people in different societies may perceive such connections very differently. Moreover, while obesity may be seen as unfortunate (and possibly sinful) by people in some cultures, many
others draw no such conclusions. That sweets have been linked
to dental decay has some basis in fact; but the pressure against
eating sweets for that reason contains no substantial moral com-
ponent. I propose to try a somewhat different route toward understanding the abnegation of sugar and other substances as immoral, by suggesting that we use feelings about obesity as a clue.
Moral feelings about the body today deeply affect how foods are
perceived, and in a manner markedly different from that which
was true three centuries ago.

SUGAR AND THE SELF

The modern individual, of whose body and needs we now speak, is the product of the Industrial Revolution and the rise of an economic system given over more and more to the gratification of individual consumption. That system has distinguished itself by its success not only in producing the consumables, but also in specifying and defining the needs.[11] Such processes of production and need-definition have stretched over nearly three centuries and continue still, ever stronger. They began to take on a modern form, I suspect, with the first commodities changed from luxuries into daily needs, including such things as tea, tobacco, and sugar, soon followed by clothing, china, and much else.

This is not to claim that ordinary working people in late eighteenth-century Britain became totally different sorts of human beings simply by becoming consumers of such substances. Nonetheless, consuming exotic products purchased with their own labor—which allowed them to see themselves as *being* different because they were able to choose to consume differently— surely helped to *make* them different. That "one is what one eats" took on new meaning, once much of what one ate became different, came from far away, and could be bought if one had the cash. No sumptuary rulings would affect sugar or tea or tobacco consumption; rather than *lèse majesté*, such consumption only made the king richer and more powerful, while enabling the consumers to consume "like a king."

In the new scheme of things, what one consumed became a changing measure of what (and of who) one was. Status did not so much define what one could consume; what one consumed helped to define one's status. The individual—a producer— came to be redefined as a consumer; her desires were continuously remodeled. Collective (social) needs would now take on a different form, altered by the expansion of individual needs, as these became more immediate, more apparent, and more widely justified in the press, by the political organs of the state, and even from the pulpit.

To reconnect morality to sugar in terms of the modern individual, it is necessary to contextualize the shaping of those individual needs over time and to try to understand the way they were experienced. The relationship between work and ensuing satisfactions becomes more intimate. Specifying satisfaction itself becomes more individual and personal. For this new individuality to take shape, society must succeed in shifting people's perceptions of where the locus of desire lies. That desire, now defined in terms of the individual, is relocated, so to speak; it acquires a voice of its own, a voice I believe to be conditioned in part by society's new ways for publicizing and elaborating what is desirable. The motor of desire, speaking now largely with its own voice, is transformed into one of the most powerful of all signals attesting to the *existence* of the individual. This highly divisible, modern self is now a "bundle of desires," elements which come together and express themselves unitarily at certain moments, probably with special clarity in acts of consumption.[12]

This conception of the individual can be aligned with the issue of food and morality and, more specifically, with the issue of sugar and morality. Then it is the *refusal to consume* that needs examination from a moral standpoint. But this construction is, as indicated earlier, qualitatively different from what precedes it. It has to do with the forgoing of sucrose in the consecration of the self. One "cuts out," "gives up," "swears off," "does without" sugar, in order to live longer and to be healthier, prettier, shapelier, and more competitive—but also to consume even more of a different kind, according to one's personal conceptions of what one can become.

Such forswearing can be done without apparent commitment to other humans, to other species, to one's own society, to other societies, or to the world—without any commitment at all, in fact, except to a newer, lovelier you.[13] But it should be apparent that the "you" in this instance is far more frequently female than male; and that the newer, lovelier you may be forged with others very much in mind. Any discussion of dieting in American society must take account of maleness and femaleness, and of its clearly gendered rendering of the female body-image. Women who diet may do so primarily to please themselves; but they do so also to make themselves members of a gender-defined group of abnegators, self-defining and self-fulfilling. Their highly individualized sacrifices validate that membership; but such sacrifices are often meant to please males as well, either in the abstract or specifically. The encouragement to consume; to consume various goods and services simultaneously;[14] to use consumption as an index of one's status; to show no interest in ceilings for consumption or, for that matter, in floors for consumption, either[15]—all militate against conceptions of the human body as a *satiable* entity. The material world, which both is, and is envisioned as being, unimaginably rich in both goods and services for those with the means to pay, is refashioned to yield infinite, not finite, satisfactions. This reconstruction developed in particular during the last century, and had the effect of changing as well the ways in which the individual is definable in relation to others.

The link between morality and sugar in the modern world must be descried against the background of an army of consumers prepared to consume messages about health, love, and beauty on the one hand; and, on the other, to repudiate large quantities of sucrose, prepared in an infinite number of ways—particularly in pruriently named desserts, but also in everything from bread and salt to salad dressing and catsup. To those who reject sucrose, the only immediately visible moral principle in this picture is that of self-discipline. But in this case the moral principle involves responsiveness to definitions of the self which may seem for the most part to omit society at large—and, for that matter, the needs of other societies or of other life-forms. It is as if the reason why individuals should forgo the consumption of sucrose is for their individual improvement: no reward but self-defined virtue.

But the self is rarely disengaged wholly from its social context. Judith Goldstein [1993] writes of a "female aesthetic community," precisely because appeals to a gendered self in modern life are based on social connections, real or imagined. It is the intent of health and beauty advertising to accentuate simultaneously the appeal of intensely self-oriented improvement by self-denial, *and* the appeal of membership thereby in some imagined group that shares elite consumerist interests.

The renunciation of certain consumables—sugar, for instance—may be accompanied by alternate or increased consumption of other things. Such renunciation generally proceeds because of self-referential (that is, individual) decisions about behavior. Also commonly involved are ideas about the ordering of lifestyle—of blazing behavioral trails to a new personality. These claims fit well with arguments advanced by Jonathan Friedman [1989], who argues that consumption under capitalism simultaneously involves individualism, consumerism, and romanticism. Before the rise of modern consumerism, Friedman thinks, the individual was embedded in networks of dependency that defined his or her identity in relation to others in the same social system: "All relations, from those within family networks, to the class structure were defined in terms of established forms of interaction and etiquette. Who one was and how one was to act were related as essence to appearance" [125]. To replace the older, more fixed system, capitalism breaks down the socially defined meaning that system provided individuals, depersonalizes the public sphere, and increases people's feelings of anonymity, of not belonging. The public and the private become acutely different. As an older social system becomes dilapidated, one's individual identity is called into question more. The use of consumption as a means to define oneself becomes commoner; the market emerges as a mirror of what one is, and what one can become. The romantic ethic, which enables the individual to pursue some different lifestyle, comes into its own by means of the market. This new sort of individual is truly different; the market has created her, by allowing her to buy her new self.

"In order to be a romantic," Friedman writes:

> ... one must endure the experience of alterity, of otherness. One must, thus, be formally alienated from any specific social reality in order to seek new realities. One must be an individual whose essence is independent of all specific social and cultural attributes. That essence becomes nature, that which is universally common to all humans, defining in its turn the typical universality of occidental discourse and its world historical outlook. [127]

The individual as a consumer who creates cultural forms by which to live and then discards them in order to create new ones accords with the repudiation of particular practices or objects (including of course foods) as a means of enhancing and intensifying individuality and distinctiveness. Such creativity does not mean reducing consumption, but molding it to accommodate changing needs and images, which are enhanced exactly because they are changing. Its romantic aspect is clear: the consumer arranges her desires in a coherent manner, both for self-definition and for novelty. Without addressing directly the estimates accorded obesity in such individual schemes, we see that consumption forgone can simultaneously satisfy differing ends.

The triad of individualism, romanticism, and consumerism fits well with the picture of a new self. The repudiation of a desired good bestows virtue, while opening the door to additional consumption of different kinds. Exercise of choice heightens the illusion of individuality. The utilization of choices of consumption to create an effect of changing form—in this instance, quite literally, changing form—fits with the romantic conception of the self. In these ways, the rejection of sugar—of tobacco, drugs, coffee, TV, cholesterol, unfiltered water, synthetic fiber, irradiated fruit, red meat, whatever—enables one to march to the beat of a different drummer, made more attractive because one can also believe one is among the first to hear its tattoo. But this individuality is conditioned by the postulation of a "group," membership in which is attainable among other things by certain consumptions of sacrifice, based on inner will—on difficult choices, freely made, to validate one's fitness for belonging. Such a "group" consists not of one's family or health club or alumni association, but of an abstraction from the pages of certain magazines and from television, generated by the best salespersons in world history. An imaginary group of this kind corresponds well with Friedman's idea of "an individual subject with no necessary socially established essence" [127]. Using the products (or, in the case of sugar, not using them) is how the imagined group is joined. By such urgings to "moral" performance, individuals learn to consume with more discipline; morality, detached from society itself, thus becomes a new consumable.

chapter six

COLOR, TASTE, AND PURITY:
SOME SPECULATIONS ON THE
MEANINGS OF MARZIPAN

In these days of heightened concern with the environment, when our water, our food, and even the air we breathe seem fragile, we human beings may think ourselves more vulnerable than our ancestors. At one time such vital features of our environment as air and water must have seemed as reliable as the sun itself. More threatening to our species were the difficulties of marshaling the necessary forces of production. But no longer.

color, taste, and purity

Now the forces of production certainly seem adequate, even if the distribution of their fruits continues to raise questions. It is the environment itself that is uncertain now. Recent history and the mass media "prepare" us for environmental catastrophe. We are ready to discover impurity at every turn, to be threatened by impurity at any moment. Much of our yearning for what is pure—water, air, vegetables, fruit—looks like nostalgia for a past ever more rapidly receding.

In view of these worries, it may be fair to ask just what we mean these days when we speak of things as "pure." Do we mean something that is natural, unaltered, unprocessed—an unspoiled product of nature's agents: the unfettered action of sun, water, air, soil, and organic growth, unaltered by the action of humankind? Or do we mean something else—something that may be equally comforting though quite different: aseptic, scientifically clean, hygienic, chemically quantifiable, free of germs and microbes, guaranteed not to make us sick?

The question is not idle. A moment's reflection reveals that both of these meanings of "pure" are correct, though they are significantly different. By "pure" we *do* mean natural, unspoiled, simple, earthy. But by "pure" we *also* mean safe, biologically cleansed, scientifically aseptic, germ-free. The contrast in meaning centers on two rather dissimilar views of nature which, perhaps oddly, many of us appear to hold simultaneously. One way to phrase this contrast would be to say that most of us put our faith in God and in Science at the same time. While that hardly seems contradictory to most people, it has surely served as the basis for contradictions. That a single term can be thus endowed with two such different meanings says something, of course, about the way we humans think. Not only are these two meanings of "pure" distinct conceptually; they are also conceptually counterposed. Nature, precisely because it is natural, is not chemically clean. But scientific purity, exactly because it is chemically clean, is not natural. This conundrum embodies a clear and unresolved conceptual polarity in our thinking.

That the concept of purity should be so complicated ought not really to surprise anyone, however. Every religious system must deal in some way or another with the problems posed by the issue of purity in the process of defining itself. No religious code has successfully solved all of those problems. And since food and eating are so commonly entangled in the specification of purity—not only *what* is pure, but also, and in relation to food, *who* is pure—it is quite easy to construct puzzles in which purity, food, and religious belief are intertwined. To food and to faith we need only add a medical dimension—definitions of illness and health, and the character of cure—to reach a point from which the concept of purity may be reflected upon, in terms of food.

By selecting a single food whose history we know at least in part, it may be possible to illustrate how ideas of purity are worked out in practice. Consider, for example, the ground almond confection called marzipan (Eng. *marchpane*, Fr. *massepain*, Ital. *marzipane*). The word itself, of much interest to philologists and historians of sugar, is thought to derive from Arabic *ma wthabân*: the sitting lord.[1] The origins of the distinctive combination of almond paste, sugar, and other ingredients, while surrounded by legend,[2] are probably Middle Eastern.

Many sweet confections were first introduced into Europe from other lands; they came from farther east. Honey and fruits had of course been known in Europe for millennia. But Islam deserves the credit for introducing intensely sweet confections made from sugar. Such delicacies reached the Europeans by two quite different routes. A ninth-century Arab manuscript from Iraq, for instance, the *Al-Tabassur bi-l-tigara* ("Concerning Clarity in Commercial Matters") describes some of the exotic goods carried westward from the area of the Persian Gulf: sugar candy from Ahwaz; fruit syrups, quince, and saffron from Isfahan; rosewater, water lily, and jasmine ointment from Fars; and candied capers from Bushehr [Mintz 1985, 97]. These were all exotic and expensive delicacies for the Europeans, luxuries for which the privileged and powerful were prepared to pay dearly. They came to the European courts mostly via the Italian port cities, and many of them were sweet.

But both sugar and almonds were by then already long known in Spain. Authorities date the introduction of the sugar cane to Spain to the Moorish conquest in the eighth century; its cultivation, and the subsequent manufacture of sugar, followed. Hence, while honey can be documented in Europe even in the late Paleolithic, sucrose made from the juice of the sugar cane entered the Iberian Peninsula with the Moors. Edward von Lippmann [1970 (1929) 240 et seq.] supposes the introduction of sugar cane cultivation there to have marked the reign of Abd-Ar-Rahman I (755–788); and though the mastery of sugar refining in the Peninsula came somewhat later, sugar confections probably became fairly common, soon after the conquest itself.

The almond had long been cultivated in Spain. It was well known and ancient in the Mediterranean region. It is frequently mentioned in the Bible; associated with the coming of spring and with fertility; and had clear mythical and religious significance in both Greek and Roman cultures. The almond tree is Central Asian in origin, but it is very old, all around the Mediterranean basin. It seems certain that the sweet almond figured in local cuisines in various ways, often in dishes that were themselves in no way sweet. Thus, for instance, unsweetened ground almonds have long been used to thicken sauces in the cuisines of the Middle East and North Africa, and this practice became common in European courts from at least the thirteenth century onward. Almonds figure importantly in the recipes of *The Forme of Cury*, that remarkable cookbook compiled by the cooks of the English monarch Richard II around 1390; and such recipes mark a late point, not an early one, in the use of almonds in cookery.

W. E. Mead, writing of medieval Europe, speaks of "the amazing consumption of almonds":

> They are boiled and stamped and sugared and served cold. They are blanched and ground, mixed with

ale and water, strained, boiled, flavored with saffron, sugar, and salt, and served hot. Almond milk, caudle of almond milk, almond butter, fried cream of almonds, are frequently mentioned as dainties to be served separately. [Mead 1967, 106]

To dramatize this usage, Mead recorded the number of recipes in Austin's *Two Fifteenth Century Cookbooks* containing almonds. Of the 153 recipes for soups (*potage*), no less than 60 contain almonds; of the meats (*leche vyaundes*), 13 of 64; of the bakemeats (*vyaunde furnez*), 10 of 41. Recipes consisting of little more than almonds include those for "Froyde Almaundys," "Fryit creme of Almandys," "Cawdel de Almaunde," "Hagas de Almondes," "Froyte de Almondes," and "Cheaut de Almondes" [Mead 1967, 106–7].

It is more difficult to make a case for the use of almonds in medicine in medieval Europe[3] than it is for sugar, whose medicinal uses I noted in the preceding chapter. As the humoral medicine of Galen and Hippocrates reentered Europe via Arab medical centers, Nestorian, Jewish, and Arab doctors employed, modified, and reinterpreted ancient practice, translating the original texts into Arabic and, eventually, into Latin. To the large pharmacopoeia of Galenic medicine, they made numerous additions, among which the use of sugar for medical purposes was undoubtedly one of the most important.

Sugar's efficacy as a medicine was widely endorsed; it turns up in the composition of every major remedy used against the Black Death. Carl Sudhoff's *Pest Books* tell us: "In none of the prescriptions is sugar lacking, added as it is to the medicines of the poor as a substitute for the costly electuaries, the precious stones and pearls, to be found in the medicines of the rich" [Mintz 1985, 100]. But it was fine white powdered sugar, not simple syrup, that was employed. The supposed effectiveness of sugar was linked to the degree to which it was refined; the whiter the sugar, the more effective it was supposed to be, medically.

color, taste, and purity

The emphasis on whiteness (which, in the case of sugar, would be correlated with the degree of its chemical purity) probably has a wider meaning, however. For example, the famous Spanish dish traditionally employed as a remedy for illness, the *manjar blanco*, was composed of breast of chicken, rice flour, milk, and sugar, all of which ingredients are white. The *blanc mangier* or *blanc manger*, which turns up in the cookbook of Philip the Fair (1268–1314), was also made of breast of chicken, to which was added almond milk, white bread, and ginger. This dish was cooked and flavored with a brew of rosewater [Lippmann 1970 (1929), 307]. These curative combinations, with their emphasis on white ingredients, suggest strongly that whiteness itself may have been thought of as inherently curative. The symbolic linkage of whiteness to purity appears to be ancient in European thought, as does the idea—much more widespread and probably much more ancient—that things that are pure can purify.

I am suggesting some possible symbolic connection, then, between whiteness and curative properties; between whiteness and purity; and between sugar and almonds. Those two ingredients are the essentials of the delicacy called marzipan. That marzipan as we know it may have an entirely Spanish history (as has often been argued, but which I am inclined to doubt) does not affect the argument here, for my concern is the relationship of the history of the composition of marzipan to the theme of purity and health.

It is commonly asserted that the sweet delicacies of Spain are each linked to particular religious orders or centers—nunneries and monasteries. To this day many sweets—including liqueurs —are associated with such centers. Though to my knowledge no historian so far has attempted to explain that association in terms of the indirect medical benefits of producers who are themselves pure and are engaged in fabricating pure products, it seems deserving of reflection.

To be sure, many or perhaps most sweet things are not (or are no longer) white. The irony, in the case of marzipan, is that once

the technique for manufacturing this delicacy was widely diffused, it achieved modern popularity because of its versatility. It
can be given any shape, any color; and its attractiveness to children rests in part on these qualities, as well as upon its sweetness.
The marzipans of Lübeck or of Milan, with their clever imita-
tions of hot dogs, animals, and all sorts of objects gain their customers in part because they are multicolored. But at a time in the
past when whiteness and purity were seen as covariants (still embodied in our wedding gowns, wedding cakes, confirmation
dresses, choices of flowers, and lexical symbols), the whiteness of
bleached almonds, almond milk, and fine sugar may be seen to
have played a part in their popularity.

The declining price of sugar, particularly after the explosive
development of the New World sugar plantations in the seventeenth century, changed the way that sugared delicacies were regarded in Europe, making them more commonplace and ordinary. No doubt they remained as wondrous as ever to children.
But those white confections, once prized for their sweetness,
whiteness, and purity, must have seemed rather less special, as
sugar itself became available in larger supply, even for the poor.

Purity, as imputed to edible white substances—in the case of
sugar and almonds, both *processed* to whiteness by human ingenuity—is remote from the purity we seek in a world now apparently suffering from an excess of human ingenuity. Yet, although
both sugar and almonds are altered through human interven-
tion, the nature of that alteration is quite different. Blanched and
ground almonds are simply blanched and ground, nothing more;
and they were a familiar food in the Mediterranean basin long
before the appearance of sugar. They might well have been seen
as a naturally pure substance. In contrast, sugar came with the
Moorish conquerors. Its processing is lengthy and complex. The
sticky, dirty sap of a tall grass, infested with plant lice and ants,
is converted by pressure and by heat, and by the addition of
cleansing agents, into a fine, powdery (or granular), and very

white substance—a chemical and mechanical transformation that still impresses the observer.

There is something contradictory about the way we humans dream on the one hand of a pure and natural world, unencumbered by the consequences of human activity, even while our desires for comfort, affluence, satiety, and physical safety constantly outpace that dream of unaffected nature. I have suggested here that the intrinsic contradiction expressed by our desires is embodied in the very language we use, as in our use of the term "pure." Most of us feel little able to affect what becomes of our world, which we often see as having changed during our own lifetimes from being "natural" to being "too scientific"—from one kind of "pure" to another. Could it be that, in its happy blending of desirable substances, marzipan represents a modest symbolic resolution of the contradiction between the two meanings of "pure"?

CUISINE: HIGH, LOW, AND NOT AT ALL

The different ways in which people in the same society can talk about food is quite striking. For instance, all of us know persons for whom the *taste* of food plays a truly minor role in their conscious perceptions. They do not think in an intent or active way about what they are eating when they eat it: not about what the food is, not about the way it tastes or smells, not about its temperature or appearance. They may not even talk about the feelings it arouses—one supposes because it arouses no feelings. They may speak about foods that "don't agree with" them, or about what foods they "can't stand." But if we try to find out how *thought* accompanies their eating, we may come up empty-handed. Such people, when asked whether what they are eating is "good," may nod their heads, or say "yes." But they are not likely to volunteer any other information, other than perhaps politely, if there is a host or cook present.

I suspect that none of us likes to think that she or he may be such a person, because it could imply a lack of acuity, or of awareness, perhaps even a coarseness of mind. But that there are many such people is, nonetheless, apparent to all of us; and some of them would say that the sort of awareness I have in mind is really effeteness, affectation, or narcissism, masquerading as refinement. But when I esteem an awareness of food, I don't mean to commend a kind of generalized thinking about food, "cultivated" thinking about food; I mean, rather, thinking about the food on our plates, and what feelings or thoughts that particular food directly gives rise to.

Intellection *about* food is a different matter. Many people who are not interested in food as food are quite interested in food as thought. I think that there is an analogy (if not a very good one) with music. Many people who know little about music or its history really do care about sounds, and have astonishing insights about the sounds they hear, even about music that they have never heard before. Sometimes such people have relative or absolute pitch, can remember tunes, even some heard long ago; and often they are startlingly open to new sorts of sounds. But others, who may know all about the Bachs, or Tchaikovsky's love life, may tend to fall asleep in their seats during a performance of *Don Giovanni*, can never bring to mind the so-called "fate" theme of the Beethoven Fifth Symphony and, when you get right down to it, may not really *like* music.

The sorts of differences among people I am talking about are clearly individual. My father and mother were as different from each other in regard to music as are the two types I have drawn above. Like music, food evokes a wide range of responses among different people, in any culture. But different cultures appear to have different ranges of variability for nearly everything, so that it would be awfully risky to generalize about the whole spectrum of food attitudes among human beings, or even about the range of possibilities within a single culture.

In spite of the variability of individual differences in this regard, there is a point in trying to link people's feelings about food in some one particular culture with the foods that people in that society customarily eat—what gets called, more or less imprecisely, its "cuisine." The meaning of that word is murky enough to merit some discussion, and that is what this chapter is mostly about. People know that the term "cuisine" is borrowed from the French language, and that it means "kitchen," among other things. Some know that it originated in the Latin verb *coquere*, to cook, which gave rise to *coquina*, and then to *cocina*, *cucina*, *Küche*, "kitchen," and so forth. Generically, "cuisine" means not just "kitchen" but also "cooking." Thus Brillat-Savarin: "La cuisine est le plus ancien des arts." The French speak of grande cuisine, of haute cuisine, of cuisine bourgeoise. But these terms, while they have dictionary definitions, are anything but precise. What I want to do here is to talk about what "cuisine" can mean: about national cuisines, regional cuisines, haute cuisine, and the possibility of a society having no cuisine. Not having a cuisine would be quite different from not having a navy, say, or not having democratic institutions. But before examining the implications of not having a cuisine, one must first figure out what a cuisine is.

In the United States, people rarely talk about "American cuisine." If the term "cuisine" is used at all here, it seems mostly to take on an ethnic or national character: French cuisine, Indian cuisine, Thai cuisine, Chinese cuisine. (This last has become dilapidated during the last two decades, as regional variants in Chinese cooking were first discovered by Americans, then largely dissolved by the relentless degradation of distinction in bad restaurants.)

Whether it makes sense to speak of a national cuisine at all is questionable. Jean-François Revel, for one, thinks not. While he concedes that there may be some grounds for talking about an international cuisine, for him the only real cuisines are regional because of the enduring distinctiveness of local ingredients [Revel 1982]. Though there may be other ways to think about a national cuisine, for any serious purpose I think Revel is right. Terms such as "French cuisine" make sense only in a manner quite different from what "cuisine" once meant. If there were a restaurant in Des Moines, Iowa, named "Gerbe de Blé" or "Les Gaulois," that vaunted a menu in both French and English, offered to prepare for its guests the drink called *kir*, used sauces such as *béarnaise* and *grenobloise*, served snails or some sort of pâté as a first course, and had a wine list with at least some wines from Bordeaux on it, we would know what kind of cuisine it has. French, of course—what else?

We can play the same game with a place called "Due Amici" in Hartford, or "Zum Brauhaus" in Milwaukee. In this sense there are "national" cuisines, because cooks from particular countries go abroad and prepare the foods they know how to make, out of the ingredients that are available, in ways resembling the ways they used back home. Or, as is more likely to be the case today, they do those things according to the recipes they learned while attending a school of cuisine, where they were trained to prepare "classic" dishes. A restaurant in a distant land with an imaginative and well-trained chef can surely provide her clientele with food that springs from some rooted culinary tradition: *tripes à la mode de Caen, ossobuco à la milanese*, Boston baked beans. These can be called signature foods because they stand for something more than themselves. Their distinctive character related at one time to cooking methods and ingredients typical of certain locales, and perhaps only obtainable there. Such foods are intimately linked to the local economy.

A talented chef with excellent food resources can prepare a menu that is nearly flawless in reflecting the foods of some nation. But the foods of a country do not, by themselves, compose a cuisine. Cuisines, when seen from the perspective of people who care about the *foods*, are never the foods of a country, but the foods of a *place*. The place may be quite large—Emilia Romagna, or Béarn, or Bavaria—but it is a geographically definable place with some sort of borders. Its size will be determined partly by social and not geographical considerations. The foods that compose its cuisine come from that place. Such foods are notably *regional*, in contrast to talk of grande cuisine or haute cuisine, which are (at least implicitly) national.

Grande cuisine and haute cuisine arise out of political and social change. Regional cuisines contribute to the appearance of a national cuisine because ingredients, cooking methods, and dishes drawn from regional cuisines become the repertory of chefs who cook for persons whose knowledge, taste, and means transcend locality. This commonly happened historically in capital cities, and at court, and of course the clients were privileged and often powerful. While a cluster of different dishes may be tantamount to a cuisine, it is not easy to speak of a national cuisine unless we have in mind the contents of a book, a restaurant, or some particular nation, in contradistinction to some other. The cuisine of Alsace, which is regional, is also "French" because Alsace lies within a national state named France. The cuisine we call French can be contrasted to the cuisine we call Italian.

I mean to argue here that what makes a cuisine is not a set of recipes aggregated in a book, or a series of particular foods associated with a particular setting, but something more. I think a cuisine requires a population that eats that cuisine with sufficient frequency to consider themselves experts on it. They all believe, and *care* that they believe, that they know what it consists of, how it is made, and how it should taste. In short, a genuine cuisine has common social roots; it is the food of a community—albeit often a very large community.

Take something as simple as bread. In France as in Italy, bread is a nearly invariant accompaniment of any meal, and people have strong feelings about how it should taste. They eat it every day, most of them at every meal. This does not mean that there is only one kind of bread or that all bread tastes the same, or that people think it should. Rather, how bread tastes, how the dough is prepared and baked, are subjects of sufficient familiarity and importance to be the basis of discourse. Such subjects unite people culturally; and they tend to do so without reference to such things as belonging to one class or another, or having this much or that much formal education. In some ways, that is what's most interesting about cuisine—when people have one, they know what it is without regard to what other people may tell them, *because* they have been eating it (and many of them, preparing it) for all of their lives, and so they can talk about it.

In the course of nation formation, some elements of the regional cuisines are likely to surmount regional distinctions (or they may predate them). Bread is probably the best European example and, accordingly, a good basic food for people to talk about, as in France or Italy. In Italy, probably pasta could serve as another example. The preparation of bread or pasta will vary from region to region, but it will nonetheless be a common, shared subject of dialogue, of conventional understandings about cooking and eating. Some vegetables may also have "climbed" from regional to national: spinach and broccoli and artichokes and eggplant in Italy; endives and carrots and string beans and celeriac in France.

I do not think this means that there is a national cuisine, though, except in the sense of an aggregation of foods, styles, cooking methods and signature dishes from the regional cuisines, based partly on better transportation and communication, and greater means. It is no secret that nations were not made in heaven, but by political and military activity. The food of the monarch's court and the court language may be created by different processes; but the political reality of the central state is what brought them both into being, in their national manifestations.

"Cuisine" in a more practical sense, though, is regional. By "practical" I mean here people using ingredients, methods, and recipes on a regular basis to produce both their everyday and festive foods, eating the same diet more or less consistently, and sharing what they cook with each other. I should add that I find it difficult to understand how a people can have a cuisine without ongoing, active producing of food and producing of opinions about food, around which and through which people communicate daily to each other who they are. Food does not have to be one of those things through which such processes of validating group membership goes on; but if it is, it is probably a "real" cuisine.

Room has to be left here to talk about those eating distinctions within a society that are not regional in origin or character, but that mark off groups from one another. In American society, we think of course of class: who eats filet mignon, and who chuck steak; who eats caviar, and who hake; who drinks blush wine and Gallo, and who Lafite Rothschild; even who goes to fast-food restaurants and who to Lutèce. But that is not so in all societies. Jack Goody, the eminent British social anthropologist, once wrote a book largely because he had encountered a mystery during his fieldwork in Africa that had to do with social distinction in cuisine [Goody 1982]. He had worked among a people in a populous, sophisticated tribal society with political leaders and substantial economic distinctions between groups—but where everybody ate just the same as everybody else. They really did. Goody was puzzled by what seemed to be an utter lack of status-based distinctions in food habits, despite the substantial other social differences that divided people. But in fact there is no reason why people *must* stratify their food habits; it's just that many cultures do, and we Americans perhaps in particular. Mary McCarthy once wrote that the striking thing about Americans eating, in contrast to Europeans, was precisely that. In Europe, she said, people at different class levels had different quantities of prized food. But the food itself was much the same, top to bottom. In the United States, in contrast, she thought different classes ate really different food.[1] I think that she was right and will try to suggest why.

cuisine: high, low, and not at all

So far what I've been talking about is "cuisine," not *haute cuisine*. It is to *haute cuisine* that I wish now to turn. Sometimes people use "cuisine" to mean "haute cuisine," as does the scholar I want to mention next, Michael Freeman, writing on Chinese food. Freeman enumerates four defining features of a cuisine. But when you read what he says, you see right away that he means *haute* cuisine:

> The appearance of a [haute] cuisine, then, involves the availability of ingredients, many sophisticated consumers, and cooks and diners free from conventions of region or ritual. A happy coincidence of developments in agriculture and commerce, related to political events and attended by shifts in attitudes about food, occurred in China during the reign of the house of Chao (960–1279) and led to a cuisine we still recognize today as Chinese.
>
> An important element, perhaps the decisive one, in the development of Chinese cooking during the Sung period was the changes in agriculture which took place then. Such changes were important, first of all, because they increased the overall food supply. [Freeman 1977, 145]

Freeman mentions (1) ingredients; (2) and (3) consumers and cooks—two different groups who aren't tied to a local food subsystem; and (4) basic shifts in people's attitudes toward food, as the four fundamentals in the emergence of an *haute* cuisine. To develop Freeman's argument, I want to suggest a hypothetical (and fictitious) anthropological example.

The eating habits and foods of the Bukurubuku, who live here, and the Abenares, who live there, are quite different. The Bukurubuku eat whale blubber, little birds, and the meat and internal organs of seals and walruses. The Abenares eat buffalo meat and fat, berries, and some wild plants. The Bukurubuku and the Abenares live in widely separated areas with different natural environments; they hunt different sorts of game, and they have different kinds of social organization and speak different languages. American anthropologists would probably all agree that the Abenares and the Bukurubuku have "different cultures." Their foods and eating habits differ from each other's as the rest of their cultures are different; that is, the level at which they are different is at the level of being different peoples with different cultures.

Internal or intrasocial differentiation of their foods—where one might find a "higher" and a "lower" level (of foods, their preparation, the ways they are served, for example) within the As or within the Bs—is a different matter. Low and high here would have to mean that there were differences we could specify in their foods or their ways of preparing and eating, or both, which distinguished one group from another *inside* the same society. However many groups there may be in one society, and whatever the aspects of foods and eating through which differences may happen to reveal themselves, "internal differentiation" only makes sense if we're talking of a single society. We can imagine without difficulty that the Abenares have taboos that keep women from eating some foods in adolescence; that certain meats are reserved for chiefs only; that male children receive extra portions of some food or other—and so on. In contrast, the Bukurubuku may be rough-and-ready democratic folk, at least when it comes to food, with everyone eating just about everything.

Of course, if one way of eating is considered "lower" than another, then there is hierarchy. Hence we think of haute cuisine or grande cuisine as being the attribute of a class or some privileged group, when we compare it to what people in that society ordinarily eat. People talking about North American food don't think that Tex Mex is high, and Bostonian low—or vice versa. But they certainly have clear ideas about better and less good food. We may also compare a society with itself at two points in time, concluding that it has acquired or lost an haute cuisine. We may say that China had an haute cuisine (many people think that nowadays it has largely survived only in Taiwan and Hong

Kong). But if we say that China has an haute cuisine, clearly we do not mean that every Chinese in China eats that cuisine.

Do we impute an haute cuisine to every society? Every society has ways for supplying people with raw materials that can then be turned into food, but the term "haute cuisine" has to mean more than that. There is self-consciousness connected with the emergence of an haute cuisine, and some sense that it transcends local difference. Do we attribute a cuisine to every society that has an haute cuisine? If there is a historical relationship between the cuisine and the haute cuisine, I think we have to. But one can also imagine a society that has no cuisine, but that has what it calls an haute cuisine, everything in it being borrowed from somewhere else. An haute cuisine need not have geographical roots; its social character is based on class. We come back to an earlier assertion: a *cuisine*, as I try to define it here, must have *social* roots, must have roots in a community.

Along what lines can the haute cuisine of a class or privileged group reveal itself? *By what it cooks and serves*—nightingales' tongues and caviar—sometimes ensured by sumptuary distinctions (only the king, or his family, or the nobility get to eat them, along with the swans and sturgeon). *By supplying things out of season*—the first fruits (*primeurs*), only the best at the season's height, the last available—sometimes enhanced by additional preparation through salting, drying, preservation, distillation, and the like (whence pears in syrup, *eau de poire* or Poire William, crystallized pears, pear nectar, pear jam—the processes to produce all of which increase the value added to the product). *By how it cooks*—number of person hours and quantities of accumulated skills (often as functions of each other) invested in each mouthful. *And by distinctive ingredients*, regionally anchored, not truly substitutable. *Baudroie* and *lotte* are not the same fish; farm salmon and wild salmon aren't, either; there's no sole like Dover sole, and so on. Repeatedly, local produce is assimilated into *haute cuisine*, though always at great cost.

Mere quantity is not all that is involved in creating a (haute) cuisine, though Freeman believes both abundance and diversity must sustain it. It is not just a matter of quantity. Nor can it be simply "how it cooks" without qualifiers: "A cuisine is surely more than the 'manner or style of cooking' of the dictionary definition; we can hardly speak of a 'short-order cuisine'" [Freeman 1977, 144]. Nor can the haute cuisine be a matter of linens, china, flatware, order of service, length of time to consume each course or the whole meal, presentation, seating, etiquette—even if such features or their analogues are likely to typify any cuisine.

Freeman begins with the availability and abundance of ingredients—surely no decisive reason for denying a cuisine to, say, the Americans. Next comes the intersection of regional cooking styles: "A cuisine does not develop out of the cooking traditions of a single region" [Freeman 1977, 144]. Here, Freeman is clearly using "cuisine" where I would use "haute cuisine" because (like Revel) I think regional cuisine is the more authentic. Next, Freeman calls for "a sizable corps of critical, adventuresome eaters, not bound by the tastes of their native region and willing to try unfamiliar food. This elite audience for good cooking must be a large one." This requirement is more serious, because it implies both travel and leisure—travel to make unfamiliar foods imaginable, then desirable because of time to do more than merely survive on them. (Trade arguably could take the place of travel, but it is unlikely to come first; until the tastes themselves have begun to be acquired, no one will import the foods that satisfy them.) As has been argued for so many other phenomena—ethnicity, for instance, and law—the appearance of an haute cuisine as opposed to "cooking" seems to hinge in part upon cultural heterogeneity, which the emerging cuisine capitalizes upon, then surmounts.

A need for variety in food may not be built into the human species, but the desire for it is suspiciously widespread. One of Freeman's final assertions seems particularly telling: "A cuisine is the product of attitudes which give first place to the real pleasure of consuming food rather than to its purely ritualistic significance" [Freeman 1977, 145]. This is a thought-provoking comment because here Freeman seems to be moving backward from the emergence of an haute cuisine to that level from which it first emerged. This claim need not be concerned with high and low, so much as with an attitude about food that presumably typifies some societies and not others. In other words, it suggests that the haute cuisine, the food of a privileged segment, arises from a broader base of food values, held by many (possibly even most) of the members of the society as a whole.

Freeman notes that technical achievements in Chinese agriculture in the Sung period increased the absolute quantities of available foods, heightened their diversity, and significantly expanded the list of foods available to ordinary people: new rice varieties, litchis, fresh fish, and the like. Tea and sugar also came into general use [Freeman 1977, 146–47]. These achievements, then, do not have to do with the perfection of an elite cuisine so much as with a general enrichment of the foodways of an entire civilization. They are neither the same as, nor mutually exclusive to, the development of an haute cuisine. Much as in France, where the attitudes and cooking habits of "ordinary" people betoken authentic cuisines, so in China one can distinguish between a culture in which food matters greatly to everyone on the one hand, and the appearance of an haute cuisine to be enjoyed by an elite, on the other. At a Chinese banquet, for instance, no rice is served, a clear signal that it *is* a banquet. But there is also a remarkable consistency from top to bottom of the society in regard to the agreed-upon ways to produce good food, and about the patterned relationships among foods, among courses, among diners. Such agreements seem to *surmount* differences in region and social rank, and this suggests that they probably *predated* the emergence of the haute cuisine. This is the only way, I think, that a social basis for a *national* cuisine can be argued.

I'm drawn back again to Freeman's assertion about "attitudes which give first place to the real pleasure of consuming food rather than to its purely ritualistic significance." Giving *first* place to the real pleasure of consuming food is, I think, a different way of saying that a widely held belief in "the real pleasure of consuming food" underlies the *cuisine*, and not just the haute cuisine. If the real pleasure of consuming food is of paramount importance to the eaters, then some elements, at least, of widespread belief about food may be necessary before an haute cuisine can be created. Admittedly this notion circumvents the question of the relation between a cuisine and an haute cuisine. But I suspect that Freeman's major assertion, that the "decisive" element in the Chinese case is substantial improvement in both food supply and variety, has to be matched by an equally decisive general "value" placed upon food as a source of sensual pleasure. Can we be confident that the hautes cuisines of Italy, France, Turkey, or China would have appeared had the masses not previously assigned a "first place" to the real pleasure of consuming food? I think that we cannot.

Only three or four basic points need to be summarized. A "national cuisine" is a contradiction in terms; there can be regional cuisines, but not national cuisines. I think that for the most part, a national cuisine is simply a holistic artifice based on the foods of the people who live inside some political system, such as France or Spain. "Cuisine," more exactly defined, has to do with the ongoing foodways of a region, within which active discourse about food sustains both common understandings and reliable production of the foods in question. Haute cuisine, so called, is some sort of refinement of the aggregate foods, styles, and dishes of a collection of regions, a skimming off of representative foods to create a cuisine that is national by virtue of being widely representative. Haute cuisine differs from cuisine by representing more than one region, by adding expensive substitutions in the foods themselves, and sometimes by acquiring international status. It is, like it or not, "restaurant food," of the sort that turns up in restaurants abroad, and in capital cities.

In cultures where food is made much of, a strong interest in how food tastes probably predates the emergence of regional cuisines. At a regional level, such interest exceeds such common foods as bread or *pasta* or vegetables, and has to do instead with fidelity to some widely held and widely understood conception of the representative foods of the region. This is, to my mind, where "cuisine" makes the most sense.

And what has this to do with what Americans eat? I try to address that question in my concluding chapter.

chapter eight

EATING AMERICAN

A year or so ago, a colleague who was teaching a course in science writing asked me to offer a lecture on food to her class. I chose as my subject aspects of the history of domestication. I regard domestication as one of the most important technical achievements in the history of our species. The lecture was well received, I thought. But in the discussion that followed, someone asked a question that had to do in part with American eating habits. When I responded, I mentioned in passing that I did not think that there is such a thing as an American cuisine. I thought nothing about it as I said it; though I had never discussed the subject with a class before, it wasn't a new idea. But in the next five minutes of the dialogue, I came to realize I had said something that some members of the class found at the least hurtful, if not downright insulting. My *gaffe* (if that is what it was) became clear almost immediately. I was asked by one student whether, since I believed we had no cuisine, I also believed we had no culture. I responded with amazement. I talked momentarily about (North) America's¹ highly regarded art, literature, drama, and poetry, claiming as I said it that our music was gradually achieving a stature equal to that we had won in these other fields. Even as I spoke I realized that the questioner was really wondering whether she had come across one of those awful persons who cannot resist running down his own country and, with her question, was just looking for proof. (I recall thinking that I had better mention some names—such as Ives, Gershwin, Bernstein, Joplin, Menotti, and Copland—in my answer, or I might be in even more hot water.) Another student took a different tack. He talked happily about "eating Thai" one night, and "eating Chinese" the next, and asked rather plaintively whether *that* couldn't be "our cuisine." He plainly felt that having access to a lot of different "cuisines" was a wonderful idea—and certainly better than meat loaf. It was all amiable enough; but I knew I'd said something a lot of people did not like to hear, nor want to believe. Before the class ended, the instructor invited students to write papers about my lecture; after a week she sent me copies of two of them, written by class members. Reading those papers made it additionally clear that I had touched a nerve. Neither paper included any comments on domestication; both talked about cuisine. If America didn't have a cuisine, these folks implied that it should; and they were certainly not prepared to accept my view of things. Though neither said it outright, I could infer that both wondered about my motives. As a consequence, I was left as interested in their sensitivity as I had been in the topic. Why, I asked myself, is having a cuisine important—is it because other people have one? Do people really think having a cuisine is like having a music, or a literature? *Is* having a cuisine like having a literature? Could it be good *not* to have a cuisine? If you don't have a cuisine, can you get one?

One reason I want to write about American eating is my eagerness to explain more clearly what I meant then. Whatever the case, it seems important to make clear that not having a cuisine is *not* like not having a literature; indeed, not having a cuisine—assuming I can make any case at all—might be a price we should be happily prepared to pay for "what's great about America."

Anyway, "eating American" is too large and too complex a subject to be tackled in this chapter, and I have to acknowledge that right away. There are a score of highly appropriate subjects I ought to raise here. But covering all those would fill another book. Still, I want to try once more to explain myself in regard to cuisine—this time, I hope, more convincingly.

When it comes to food, grasping our particularity as a nation requires us to get some sense of where our history differs from that of other countries, especially European countries.[2] The United States is extremely large in area and population, when compared to any European country but Russia. Even in this hemisphere, only Brazil and Canada are about as big, and neither is as populous. These are two obvious ways in which we differ from most places. We are predominantly European in origin, and mostly Protestant in religion. Of course we are also a young country by European historical standards—about two centuries (or seven generations) old.

The whole New World stands apart from the Old, especially from Europe, because its vast areas, as well as the aboriginal peoples who occupied them, came to be dominated by relatively small populations, and in the recent past. The conquerors mostly came from a confined but important area of the Old World: Western Europe. In terms of numbers, during the first two centuries or so, it seems likely that more Africans entered the New World than did Europeans; but their population did not grow in place as fast as did that of the Europeans; and they were almost entirely powerless, as were the indigenous peoples of the hemisphere. Hence, though Africans certainly figured importantly in the conquest and its aftermaths, though they were later joined by substantial migrant Asian populations, and though some native peoples of the hemisphere survived the impact, the Europeans were the powerholders. Their overlordship was achieved in the course of less than two centuries. Spanish and Portuguese domination, from what is the Southwest of the United States today to Tierra del Fuego, was largely in place by 1700. The insular, Caribbean region was divided up among five powers, all warring upon Spanish hegemony. That other New World areas farther north took longer to become colonial was as much a function of European wars as it was of any serious indigenous resistance.

In effect, seven nations—and to a large extent, people from those seven nations only—predominated in the conquest: Spain, Portugal, Britain, France, the Netherlands, Denmark, and Sweden. Norway, Germany, and Italy were not yet countries; but in the eighteenth century, German migration to the hemisphere was substantial, and in the nineteenth, so was Scandinavian, Italian, and East European migration. By the end of the eighteenth century, the United States had become a sovereign state, the hemisphere's first. Most Americans at the start of the nineteenth century were white and North European in origin. What the United States fully shares with many of its New World neighbors is its newness as a nation, and its being composed almost entirely of the descendants of migrants, coming from elsewhere. We share with Canada, Chile, Argentina, Uruguay, and perhaps Costa Rica the background fact that the vast majority of today's inhabitants are descended from migrants who came from Europe.

A particularly cruel consequence of conquest was the runaway depopulation of immense areas, due to the combined effects of disease, war, enslavement, and inhuman labor practices. The early movements of Europeans and Africans to the hemisphere were soon followed by others; and that movement of new peoples, especially to the United States, has literally never ceased. Except, of course, for the descendants of Native Americans— anciently descended themselves, in turn, from migrants from

Asia—all North Americans are originally from somewhere else, particularly from Europe.

In the United States immigration continued apace during the nineteenth and twentieth centuries. While its volume relative to the settled population has declined, the absolute numbers have remained high; and in the last half century, the origins of the newcomers have become much more diverse. Immigration laws in the nineteenth century had been aimed at maintaining the ethnic structure of United States society as it was then constituted, largely North European; only since World War II was that bias modified legislatively. The pace of continued immigration, while shared with some other hemispheric nations, is another relevant marker of North American distinctiveness.

At the same time that immigration has continued, national history has been marked by steady territorial expansion. The Louisiana and Gadsden purchases, the purchase of Alaska, the Spanish American War, the acquisition of Hawaii, Puerto Rico, the Virgin Islands, American Samoa, for example, and the North American imperialist policies these military conquests and purchases represented, all played a part. But while Europeans were migrating to colonial areas such as Canada, South Africa, and Australia, in our case migrant Europeans were coming to what was already a sovereign and democratic country—becoming citizens as well as inhabitants. In each instance of additional expansion, there followed further settlement, as in Hawaii and Alaska, Puerto Rico, and the (U.S.) Virgin Islands. This expansion and incorporation is another distinctive feature of United States society worthy of mention here. In most of the Americas, people who came from elsewhere had their future quite firmly charted for them by their class status on arrival; in the United States, that was not so much the case. Public education, expanding economic opportunities, and the openness of the political system produced unexpected and dynamic results.

Since its establishment as a nation, the United States has been marked by a high degree of mobility, above all geographical. Expansion westward meant a spreading out and filling up of the country as it grew. Such expansion involved military, then cultural, aggression against Native Americans, a part of our history which has come to be acknowledged publicly, more and more. Less noticed has been the enormous long-term benefit of seemingly infinite land resources for farming and, even more, ranching—a steadily dwindling treasure upon which the nation has battened for centuries, and the presence and availability of which has profoundly affected the way our eating habits (and other habits) have taken shape.

From early on, this was a highly mobile country not only occupationally, but also economically. Perhaps upward mobility is particularly noticeable when the rising group includes newcomers. Today, the bankers, generals, CEOs, and members of Congress in this country who have recent foreign forebears are legion. This makes us different and, in the eyes of, say, Englishmen of Germans, it may also make us seem rather undiscriminating. Imagine the German army with its top general a child of Turkish immigrants! Or the British army led by a child of Pakistani immigrants!

From the end of the eighteenth century onward, different regions of the new land called the United States gave rise to somewhat different diets. One reason for these differences was the wide variation in natural environments—the Southwest versus the Gulf Coast versus New England versus the Northwest Pacific, for example. Another was the differing food habits of various migrant groups. Broad differences between, say, New England cooking and Southern cooking can certainly still be sketched in. On a narrower canvas, we can speak of "Cajun" cooking, say, or "Pennsylvania Dutch" cooking, and still have it mean something. In the Midwest, some Scandinavian culinary traditions were established; in large Eastern cities, Italian and East European cooking habits took hold. To these older patterns have been added numerous others since World War II, of which Asian foods and cooking methods, only poorly represented in this country before, are the most visible, though not the only ones.

Yet such variety does not equal a cuisine, and is not the same as a cuisine. There are at least two reasons why such an assertion may seem unwarranted. On the one hand, there do appear to be *regional* cuisines, of the sort mentioned in chapter 7, which I described as the only "real" cuisines, anyway. On the other, I have contended that national cuisines are not cuisines in the same sense. So I must explain myself.

Since our beginnings as a nation, Americans have sought ways to integrate and assimilate newcomer populations within some generalized American culture. Though prejudice against both African Americans and American Indians (and in its more recent forms, toward other nonwhite populations as well) has militated against that process, most newcomers have been encouraged to forgo their traditional cultures in order to "become American." What this means is not always so clear. But the public educational system, above all, and the tremendous power of peer pressure, working on both children and adults, has helped to reshape the behavior and outlook of successive generations of new arrivals.

Several different things are happening at once. More people coming from different places continue to arrive. They are subject to pressures to change their ways, including their foodways, by an Americanization process that goes on in the schools, in the media, and in the course of daily life. The demands of new jobs and new lifestyles, and the desires and claims of the children of migrants, put great negative pressure, great pressure to change, upon older, imported standards. Geographical and socioeconomic mobility accompany these new pressures. We are not surprised to find Hmong tribespeople in Montana, Vietnamese fishermen in Texas, Sikh and Korean storekeepers in California. In many different ways, some subtle and some obvious, these people are changing their behavior and, unbeknownst even to themselves, some of their values as well, as they "become American." How these migrants may identify themselves culturally is not in dispute, particularly if they continue to use their native language; but the cultural identity of their children is a different issue and likely to be changing rapidly.

That there are powerful pressures toward sameness, working particularly upon children, may be thought to increase the homogeneity of American food habits. Such foods as hot dogs, hamburgers, ice cream, and pizza are integral to acceptable adolescent behavior, regardless of origins; young people are intensely aware of it. In a certain way, then, these pressures do push toward homogeneity. But while learning to eat ice cream, and at fast food and ethnic restaurants, has the effect of increasing homogeneity of a kind, this experience is not the same as learning, or creating, a cuisine. Strictly speaking, by learning such behavior people are becoming sociologically more alike, but it is not really clear that they are becoming culturally more alike.

Americans eat out at ever-higher levels of frequency, and barring serious economic contractions, that trend will continue. At this point, nearly one-half of the money spent on food is spent on eating out. But we have little data on how eating-out patterns vary by class. It seems to me that eating out could only be cuisine-related if if means Japanese-Americans were going to Japanese restaurants, and Italian-Americans to Italian restaurants. But in such a case, we wouldn't be speaking about an American cuisine, but about the "national" cuisines of other nations, being eaten by persons historically descended from immigrants from those nations. Sociologically, that doesn't seem important at all, especially because the people doing it would probably not think of it that way. At the same time, I don't think that there is a reliable manner in which to speak of unhyphenated Americans going to unhyphenated American restaurants to eat American cuisine, because I believe that what they eat cannot be convincingly described as cuisine.

Of course we can describe what is eaten in culinary terms, and that may be adequate for some readers. What would the cat-

egory include? Certainly hamburgers, and probably Southern
fried chicken, and clam chowders and baked beans, steak, ribs,
and perhaps chili, and hot dogs, and now, pizza, and baked potatoes with "the works." We would have a dessert list beginning
with apple pie, and we could have many dishes based on maize.
But there is no need to enumerate here all of the dishes that
might be on the list because there are so many good American
cookbooks that do the job, and no end of irrepressible enthusiasts.[3] Despite those things, however, the list of ten favorite lunch
and dinner "entrées" for 1994, collected by the NPD market research group, starts off with pizza and ham sandwiches and hot
dogs, and ends with cheese sandwiches, hamburger sandwiches,
and spaghetti. I don't think anyone wants to call that array a
cuisine.

Of the items on any more serious list, nearly all of the dishes
would be assignable to regional cuisines, which is as it should be:
all so-called national cuisines take from regional cuisines. The
maize dishes, lobsters and terrapins, the steaks and pork roasts,
the Boston baked beans, soft shell crabs and Manhattan clam
chowders would all deserve to be here. But regional cuisines
in the United States have undergone great change in the last
half century, most of it diluting or modifying the cuisines themselves. The destruction of native stocks of such foods as salmon,
shad, striped bass, terrapin, and crabs has seriously undermined
regional cuisines, for instance. But even more has been done
to change them by commercialization, a major debilitating influence.

Local variation in cuisine is under continuous pressure from
commercial enterprise aimed at profiting by turning into a national fad every localized taste opportunity. Any natural product
that is available in a place or a season, and any distinctive cooking
or flavoring method, excites merchants, packers, and processors
intent on broadening their market. Of course not all of the products travel, and many do not travel well. In the view of food busi-
nessmen it makes good sense to alter the nature of such goods in

order to make them available elsewhere, even if they no longer are (or taste like) what they were at home. In the course of the "development" of these new goods, their character is altered, and the manner in which they had been prepared is likely to be modified—more commonly, simplified or abandoned. In many cases the new product is no longer the same as the old product, and is prepared in new ways, which are reduced and cheapened versions of the old ways. What happened in recent years with "blackened redfish" is a fair example: swift vulgarization of its preparation, substitution of other fish for redfish, cheapening of the recipe, and another fad soon forgotten. The regional foods most likely to remain more authentic are exactly the ones that cannot be shipped, or do not travel well, or are either difficult or impossible to copy. But not surprisingly, that they are difficult or impossible to copy has never discouraged a North American food salesman. Hence certain foods that are regionally distinctive become known to people elsewhere who have never eaten them except in the form of substitutes lacking any resemblance at all to the original.

Such bowdlerization of food is still less frequent in Europe and elsewhere. While restaurants in Northern Germany may vaunt their Bavarian dishes, retail food markets are not likely to sell modified variants of Bavarian food. The same is true for France, and indeed for all of Europe. While one can eat *bouillabaisse* in a Paris restaurant that resembles *bouillabaisse* in Marseille, the retail food stores of Paris do not yet offer Parisians a *bouillabaisse* "exactly like the one you ate in Nice, that you can now make at home—and in just minutes!" To be sure, perhaps they soon will, so strong are the pressures to "modernize." But I suspect that commercialization of this sort has been especially effective in the United States because we lack a standard cuisine against which to test the sales pitch. Given our heterogeneous origins, with what do we compare a new food, when deciding whether to try it (or, for that matter, whether we like it)?

It is easy to romanticize the food of other cultures, and to underemphasize worldwide trends toward Westernized food patterns. We Americans are probably not so exceptional as I may seem to make us out to be. But in much of the world the food repertory is still more closely tied to seasonal availability. There are still large populations subsisting on foods drawn from a relatively narrow geographical region. In many vast areas elsewhere there are peoples who still cook in more and eat out less than we, and whose diet contains one or several staple foods eaten every day, perhaps even at every meal. Such people are differently equipped to judge any new food from most of us.

By "most of us" I mean here literate Americans of the middle class, probably with some college education, travel experience, and familiarity with ethnic restaurants. We are not given to judge each food novelty against a background of commonly recognized foods that we all eat frequently. We tend to try new foods, seeking novelty in eating, as we do in so many aspects of life. We are inclined to identify that novelty with knowingness, with sophistication; and certainly being open to new experience is a good value, most of the time. Because of our openness and the dynamism of the food vendors, in the United States in recent years consumers have learned about hummus, falafel, bagels, "designer" coffees, coriander, basil, arugula and radicchio, Jerusalem artichokes, jicama, quinoa, buckwheat groats, new rice varieties (jasmine, arborio, basmati), lactose-free milk, scones and other sweet breads (not sweetbreads!), breads baked with ingredients such as tomatoes or olives, a staggering variety of capsicums, soy milk, tofu and dried soy products, previously neglected seafoods such as monkfish, "artificial" crabmeat (surimi), and many subtropical fruits, such as mangoes, soursops, red bananas, and star apples, and a dizzying number of packaged foods designed to relieve our worries, especially about fiber and fats.

We may each individually decide which items in this cornucopia we like, and which we do not like. Some of us may even take up cooking or using one or another of them in our meals at home. If so, such foods will not be jostling with our cuisine; they will be jostling with our quiche, our pasta, our chicken breasts, our hamburgers, our peanut butter-and-jelly sandwiches, our barbecues, our steaks, our ham sandwiches, and our yogurt. These are among the things we eat the most. We can, if we wish, call them our cuisine.

As suggested earlier in this book, I do not see how a cuisine can exist unless there is a community of people who eat it, cook it, have opinions about it, and engage in dialogue involving those opinions. This is not to say that people cannot debate the merits of various restaurant renderings of *quesadillas* or *chao dze*; but that is not the same as having a cuisine. On the one hand, then, the regional cuisines of which we may speak have tended to lose some of their distinctiveness in the dilution and "nationalizing" of regional specialties. On the other, I do not believe that any genuine national cuisine has emerged as yet from this process. We do have a list of favorite foods, which we eat all of the time, and that list is broadly representative nationally; I have already enumerated most of it.

What, then, does typify American eating habits? It is clear that class, regional, and ethnic differences profoundly affect differences in eating behavior. A noticeable number of Americans now seek organically grown fruits and vegetables. About 7 percent of the nation is said to be vegetarian. Many people eat along lines prescribed by religious identity; others—but nowhere near so many as we may think—take considerations of health very seriously in the way they eat. There are also differences at the group level which betray class origins or class prejudices. In alcoholic choices, the attention paid to bread, the label-reading habit, the intense concern about weight, the sympathy toward vegetarianism, and the respect given "foreign" foods, some segments of the American middle class exhibit difference. But for the majority of the American people (including many in the above list), the following features are probably correct: eating out frequently, often choosing fast foods, as well as ordering take-out food to eat at home; eating much prepared and packaged foods, which require only intense heat or nothing at all to be "cooked"; continuing to eat diets high in animal protein, salt, fats, and processed sugars, low in fresh fruits and vegetables; drinking more soda than tap water; and consuming substantial quantities of labeled (low fat no cholesterol fat free lots of fiber no palm oil good for you) foods, packaged to encourage the consumer to feel less guilty about what he is really choosing to eat.

This list is discouraging and negativistic; of course not everyone eats this way, or all of the time. But it is worth pondering the fact that food labeling, and considerable publicity about healthier eating, have not significantly affected food habits nationally, at least not yet. The ten major sources of calories in the United States diet, according to the Department of Agriculture, are whole and low-fat milk; white bread, white flour, rolls, and buns; soft drinks, margarine, and sugar; and ground beef and American cheese. Such a list is worrisome, at the very least on health grounds, especially because of the fats and sugars. But if you are a reader who reacts by saying to herself "But I never eat *any* of that stuff!"—then ask yourself who does.

The importance of sugar and fats in the American diet is striking, particularly in view of the educational efforts to warn people of the need for moderation in these regards. During the twentieth century in this country, increases in fats and sugar consumption have accompanied a progressive decline in the consumption of complex carbohydrates [Cantor and Cantor 1977; Page and Friend 1974]. Carbohydrate consumption in the years 1910 to 1913 was two-thirds potatoes, wheat products, and other such "starchy" foods, and one-third sugar, the so-called "simple carbohydrate." By the nineties, however, the share of complex carbohydrates was down to half, that of sugars up to half. Over time, more and more of what was left of complex carbohydrate consumption took the form of deep-fried, salted, and sweetened particles, so much so as to produce a special name, "munchies," for such foods. Though there are annual variations in fat and sugar consumption, both average figures have remained high since the end of rationing after World War II. In 1991, Americans consumed 164.9 pounds per person of sweeteners, and of those, 140.6 pounds were calorie-carrying (as opposed to noncaloric) sweets. If the Institute of Shortening and Edible Oils is right in their estimate that fats consumption (in meat and dairy, and in bottles and packages—that is, both "visible" and "invisible" fats) for 1993 was 137 to 138 pounds, then when combined with caloric sugars the total fats and sugars figure is 277.6 pounds per person per year. While this figure is based on disappearance statistics (thus probably overestimating actual consumption), it is nonetheless astonishingly high. The secular shift toward fats and sugars has been accompanied in turn by significant increases in the average weights of both men and women. Many authorities now estimate one in three Americans to be twenty or more pounds—that is, clinically—overweight. The implications for health and health costs of these statistics are now so well known that there is no need to review them here.

Americans also continue to increase the frequency with which they eat out, and the frequency with which they eat in fast-food restaurants. The numbers are interesting: in 1993, 6 percent of total per capita income was spent by Americans in restaurants; only 7.2 percent—1.2 percent more—was spent on food eaten at home. (Incidentally, spending only 13.2 percent of total income on food is an astonishingly low figure, when compared worldwide.) Eating out, Americans had 793,000 "eating places" (including here not only hot dog stands, but also army mess halls) to choose from; and in them they spent 276 billion dollars.

While individual customers choose freely what they eat, they must do so in terms of what the food service offers. Eating out reduces the individual's ability to choose the *ingredients* in her food, even though it may increase the length of the menu from which she can choose. The tendency to snack remains important in American eating habits; indeed, some weakening of the luncheon pattern may be attributable to the strengthening of the morning and afternoon "breaks" [Mintz 1982], with the effect of making fast food at noon a more attractive option. In 1993 snack food sales reached a gross of nearly fifteen billion dollars. Drink patterns in 1994 were consistent: 49.6 gallons of soft drinks, followed by 31.3 gallons of tap water, 26 gallons of coffee, 22.5 gallons of beer, and 19.1 gallons of milk.

The Department of Agriculture predicted a rise in per capita beef consumption in 1995, following 1994's 67.3 pounds. Beef consumption dipped in the years 1991 to 1993, but it is now rising again. Pork consumption is also expected to rise, as is chicken. Pork consumption had dipped slightly in 1990 to 1991, but it rose again in 1992 and has stayed up; chicken consumption has simply continued to rise steadily. Increases in meat consumption are paralleled by increases in the consumption of low-fat products—*any* low-fat products. Nabisco's Snackwells, with sales of 400 million dollars in 1994, are a glowing illustration. This seemingly contradictory behavior tends to substantiate an earlier assertion: people are both eating what they feel they want and buying other foods in order to feel less guilty. They're eating *them*, too.

The dizzying overdifferentiation of food actually increases sales enormously and, as I have pointed out elsewhere, is rationalized as giving the consumer what she wants:

> Making the product "right" for the consumer requires continuous redefinition and division of the groups in which he, as an individual consumer, defines himself. The deliberate postulation of new groups—often divisions between already familiar categories, as "pre-teens" were created between "teenagers" and younger children—helps to impart reality to what are supposedly

new needs. "New" foods, as in the sequence skim milk:half and half:light (table) cream:heavy (whipping) cream split differences in order to create new needs. New medicines, as in the treatment of daytime headaches and nighttime headaches or daytime colds and nighttime colds, do the same. [Mintz 1982, 158]

In all of the processes connected with American eating, the element of *time* is extremely relevant, yet barely noticed. When Americans speak of "convenience" in regard to food, they also mean time. It is simply assumed by most of us that we have too little time. I have argued elsewhere that the insistence upon the shortness of time and the pressures of busyness in American life is in one sense completely spurious. Americans are repeatedly told that they do not have enough time, I think because it serves to increase their aggregate consumption. Doing several things at once is touted as evidence of leadership; but what it does for the economy is to increase consumption. People are supposed to be able to drink coffee and talk on the telephone while they drive, smoke while they read, and listen to music while they exercise. Vaunting such skill makes good corporate advertising sense; people use up more stuff that way. No one seems impressed by the fact that Mozart didn't chew gum or watch TV while he was writing piano concertos.

As with anything else, not having the time to eat is a function of how much time is thought to be needed for other things. To take the easiest example, Americans would have more time to cook and to eat if they spent less time watching television. The shortness of time is in many ways, then, a coefficient of a view that our time is in short supply, but also already appropriately distributed. Most "convenience food" is successful because of prior conceptions about time. But much such food would not succeed if Americans cared more about how and what they ate. That they do not is a fact of great importance; it implies not only that they lack a cuisine, but also that they probably will never have one.

What does the American future hold, so far as eating is concerned?

In a series of brilliant recent papers, Cornell University scientist David Pimentel and his colleagues have predicted sweeping changes in American agriculture, and hence in American eating patterns over the next half century.[4] Indeed, the changes that these scientists forecast, if they do occur, will be more radical in their effects on American eating than even those of the last half century—which is to say a very great deal. Demographic, agricultural, and other factors enter in. Pimentel and his colleagues, working from present trends, predict a doubling of the national population by 2064; a reduction in arable land (through both erosion and urbanization) in the neighborhood of 180,000,000 acres, or 38 percent, in the same period of time; and a total exhaustion of national fossil fuel resources in not more than two decades. The figures on rapidly diminishing water supply are similarly worrisome.

This is an unbelievably grim scenario. If it eventuates, food exports (now calculated at an average of about $155 per person per year, given our present population) would be reduced to zero. For Americans, food costs would increase by a factor of between three and five—at worst, up to more than half of total income. Should these calculations prove correct, however, the *composition* of the American diet would also have to change substantially. While nearly two-thirds of the national grain product of the United States, grown on over 100 million acres, is now used as livestock feed, by 2060 all of it would have become food for us, not for our cattle and pigs and poultry. In effect, Pimentel sees North Americans coming to eat as most of the rest of the world eats, with meat representing a much reduced fraction of our total caloric and protein intake. Since India's nearly one billion people and the People's Republic of China's even larger population get 70 to 80 percent of their calories and nearly all of their protein from grains and legumes, such a change in the United

States would be in the direction of aligning North American consumption with that of the rest of the world. It would also contribute to a vast improvement in American health. Substantial farmland could be returned to agriculture; the number of bypass and cancer operations would certainly decline.

But will it happen? As I write, McDonald's looks ahead to a rapid expansion of its enterprises in such places as the People's Republic of China, where it aims to add 600 retail establishments in the next decade; and Japan, where it now boasts more than a thousand. Whatever the scenario for the United States, many companies are working hard to spread our way of eating worldwide. Nor is there evidence that many Americans are much concerned, either about our fossil fuel consumption or our diet. Driving cars and eating meat are highly valued acts; though both involve the expenditure of unimaginably large quantities of water, soil, cereals, and fossil fuel, there is no collective indication that anyone is deeply concerned. Only sudden shortages reveal, as if in lightning flashes, how deeply held such consumption values are; Operation Desert Storm was a case in point. Indeed, one "solution" to the Pimentel prophecies is war. Successful aggression could keep meat and gas available and affordable, at least for a good while longer. Its effects on American moral integrity would be utterly disastrous. But the enormity of the decisions involved in such trade-offs would not be clearly grasped until *after* the decisions were made. There is a real trap in our not separating what we are free to do, but need not do, if it is a bad idea— from what we cannot help doing, *even though* it is a bad idea, because we think someone is trying to stop us from doing it.

No one can look down the road and predict how the American people will behave, fifty years from now. One sinister prophecy is embodied in the words of Josef Joffe, the editorial page editor of *Süddeutsche Zeitung*, who writes: "It is profligacy—being hooked on the sweet poison of consumption—that might yet lay low the American economy and thus American might."[5] But the worry is not that we will let our consumption gluttony destroy our economy; it is, rather, that we might let our obsessive notions of individual freedom destroy our democracy. The long-term lessons of our economic and agricultural policies are there to be learned now. But we have to be willing to learn them.

Notes

1. Introduction

1. See, for example, Malinowski 1935 and Firth 1957.
2. But apparently not only there. In his short story entitled "Sugar Babies," the Nigerian writer Chinua Achebe [1973] skillfully builds a story with a moral out of the scarcity of sugar in war-torn Nigeria.

2. Food and Its Relationship to Concepts of Power

1. See, for example, Elias 1978.
2. For a different view, see Pendergrast 1993.

3. Tasting Food, Tasting Freedom

1. As one Puerto Rican ex-slave once put it to me when I asked him about

125

"the slaves": "*Esclavos, no—cautivos!*" The differences between the enslaved and those born into slavery are still not well enough understood, nor their significance measured.

2. Richard Pares, a careful historian, has written:

> Many colonies made no laws at all about the feeding of slaves before the humanitarians forced them into it at the end of the eighteenth century; and even where there were laws, the standards which they enforced were pitiably low. The French *code noir* stipulated for a supply of protein which would amount to little more than a kipper a day; and this *code* was not at all well observed. Some planters normally gave their slaves no food at all, but fobbed them off with payments of rum wherewith to buy food, or with Saturdays and Sundays to till their own provision grounds and feed themselves. The rum was drunk, the Saturdays and Sundays encroached upon or wasted, and the slaves starved. Their masters almost wholly disregarded their need for protein, and could not see why they went on hunger strike, or lost their sleep catching land crabs, or died. [1960, 39–40]

A somewhat hidden debate of a most interesting sort concerns the attitudes of the slaves themselves when they stole food. On the one hand, there is the argument that the slaves, who were acquiring "Western" values, felt morally compromised by their own thievery [Genovese 1972]. The opposing (but I believe much more convincing) view is that the slaves well understood that it was their labor that was being stolen and believed that their claiming something back by "theft" was socially just [Lichtenstein 1988].

3. Unanticipated by masters, as well as by slaves. The difficulty with labels such as "resistance" and "accommodation" is the unproven explanations and the claims of motive they may carry. The cook who put ground glass in the master's family's food (resistance?) had first to become the family cook (accommodation?) [Mintz 1971a, 321].

4. Douglas Hall has evidence that the breadfruit was being planted in the garden of a Mr. Thistlewood in Jamaica seven years earlier [Hall 1988]; and the breadfruit had been present in the French Antilles *before* that time.

5. A similar tripartite division—"*les distributions*," "*les jardins particuliers*," "*la stabilisation des cultures vivrières: 'les vivres communs'* "—is employed by Gabriel Debien [1964] in describing slave foods on the plantations of the French Antilles in the seventeenth and eighteenth centuries.

6. As suggested earlier, I believe that it is not useful to divide slave acts into "accommodation" and "resistance." Some acts with consequences that can be read as resistance did not originate with resistance. Some acts

with consequences that can be read as accommodation did not originate with accommodation. Maintaining provision grounds or retailing produce in markets may be accommodation *and* resistance. The work of interpretation is far from being completed, but study of the subject is now much in vogue.

7. See, for example, Lopez 1948; Mintz 1955, 1958, 1961a, 1978a, 1978b, 1989; Mintz and Hall 1960; Paget n.d.

8. See Sturtevant 1969. From the liquid residue of processed manioc is made the stew base called cassareep (from Cariban *ḳasaripo*). Beckwith [1928, 37] says it is used to prepare the soup called "pepper pot":

> a kind of vegetable soup composed of a leaf or two of cabbage, callalu [a green vegetable now generalized to apply to any edible green leaf—from the Peruvian Spanish *ḳararú*, cognates of which can now be found occurring in some African languages], young chocho vine [*Sechium edulis*, a Caribbean cultigen], pumpkin, broad and sugar beans, tomato, and ochra, boiled with salt beef or pork and flavored with red peppers such as grow in every peasant's yard.

The importance of cassava "bread" in the region was once so great that it need hardly be mentioned here.

9. In one instance, I collected over thirty named varieties of sweet potatoes (*Ipomoea batatas*) in a relatively small area of southern Haiti and discovered that many local people could distinguish most of them readily, referring to their taste or texture, among other features. This should not be surprising. Not long ago many Americans apparently thought that all raw fish tasted the same; now some of those same Americans can distinguish raw tuna from raw salmon by their different textures.

10. If one examines Cassidy and LePage's *Dictionary of Jamaican English* [1980], for instance, it is remarkable to see how much of it is taken up with flora and fauna, with words for plants and foods. Except for the lexicographers (and sometimes, even for them), the popular language of food is subterranean; yet its forms speak eloquently to the complexity of social life.

11. Douglas Hall recounts in illuminating detail the activities of small settlers in Jamaica in the eighteenth century. Many owned slaves who were excellent gardeners. One Thistlewood, working with his slaves in February, 1768, planted "narcissi, tulips, lucerne, clovers, timothy grass, sainfoin, turnips, cabbages, parsley, borage, burnett, angelica, and many others." In October, 1770, he planted in a provision-ground, in addition to the usual food staples, potato slips, sugar beans, and alligator pear seeds. In July, 1774 (it was a Saturday), he recorded, "Gave my negroes today [i.e., to work on their own account]. Gave them

plenty of cabbage, savoy and broccoli plants to plant in their grounds" [Hall 1988, 12].

12. For instance, Price [1966] cites Père Labat's rhapsodic description of the slave who would "take orders" each morning, before going off to sea to fill them for dinner. In both Jamaica and Haiti, people today eat a small edible mushroom (*junjo* in Jamaica, *djondjon* in Haiti). It is a prized ingredient in Haitian rice. In Jamaica, such edible fungi are considered poor food—but food—as suggested by the proverb "Yo po' fe meat, unu nyam junjo" ("If you have no meat you eat [make do with] junjo" [Beckwith 1928, 37].

13. There is no end of examples; here are two.

Boiled cornmeal mush is usually known by names that are African in origin (for example, Puerto Rican, *funche*; U.S. Virgin Islands, *funji*; Haitian Creole, *akasan*), but cornmeal is, of course, American in origin. In some African cuisines, a similar mush or porridge was made from the nontoxic cassava; but that plant, too, is American in origin. Deep-fried fritters (*frituras* in Puerto Rico, and commonly known in Jamaica as *akra*) are made from black-eyed peas (the *samsa* of Haute-Volta), but the term is applied to fritters made of other substances elsewhere. In Guadeloupe, for instance, *acrats* are composed of a batter made from grated tuber, usually the so-called cocoyam, tannier, or dasheen (*Colocasia esculenta*), which is one of several Oceanian species called taro, and which reached the Antilles via West Africa. Since recipes do vary in this manner in any large geographical area, there is nothing surprising about the Caribbean situation. But it should be clear how risky it is to label a food "Eskimo" because Eskimos eat it, or something like it.

In Haiti I collected Creole terminology for animal body parts, cuts of meat, and cooked foods made from the meats. These lexicons were of interest among other things because they showed that terms of African origin were concentrated in the cooked foods category. I do not know the explanation, but I can make a guess. In both the animal name and anatomical categories, French lexicon prevailed. But when the slaves were able to cook their own food, their own names for the various dishes reappeared. One reason why such an explanation is of interest—if it is correct—is because of the light it might throw upon what is supposed to have happened in Norman England. There, the names for the prestigious foods were those taken over into English—beef, mutton, pork, for instance—from French. In the Haitian case, it was the more ordinary, even the despised, foods that ended up with African names, even when the foods were eaten by the masters. In each case, though, one might say that the lexicon was "pruned," so to speak, by social process.

14. See, for example, Handler and Lange 1978.

4. The Conquest of Honey by Sucrose

1. However, beginning in 1740 it was cut with water "so as to reduce drunkenness and crime" [Sheridan 1974, 346–47].
2. I have provided a fuller story of the parts they played in Mintz 1985.

5. Sugar and Morality

1. I am unable to establish that there is no society in which this is *not* true; and there are a great many societies. Prof. Gerd Spittler of the University of Bayreuth has argued eloquently, in the case of the Kel Ewey Tuareg, that at least one common feature of human eating habits is absolutely insignificant among them: variety. Though their diet varies at several passage ceremonies (birthdays and wakes, for example) and on Islamic holidays, the Kel Ewey otherwise eat the same rather Spartan meals every day, and do so with joy. When Spittler told them that tourists to whom he had given their food were unimpressed, they reacted by saying those were people who didn't know what tasted good. See Spittler 1987 and Spittler 1993.
2. Examples of food-related practices of indulgence, abstention, and other culturally linked variants are innumerable. The fasting by Plains Indians during the vision quest; fasting for Lent, Ramadan, and the Day of Atonement; the special significance of the Eucharist; the taking of communion as a form of eating; and truly endless other cases substantiate food's serviceability as a sphere of "marked" behavior.
3. A particularly good example is provided by Audrey Richards, arguably the best anthropologist of food who ever lived. In her *Hunger and Work in a Savage Tribe* [1932], Richards devotes an entire chapter to food and family sentiment [pp. 36–84].
4. I say this because the research needed to develop an informed picture of how British consumers of different classes actually felt about the foods they were eating in different centuries is yet to be done. I am convinced that more data are available than have yet been plumbed or classified.
5. Lippmann 1970 (1929), 329; Mintz 1985, 99. I shall not attempt to deal here with another theological principle: *Liquidum non frangit jejunum* (A liquid does not break the fast), so important in the spread of the hot

stimulant beverages, particularly chocolate, during the seventeenth century.

6. Some readers may wonder why the boycotting of sugar was not paralleled by similar boycotts on other West Indian produce. In fact sugar (with molasses and rum) was far and away the most important slave-produced commodity there, and so the abolitionists concentrated on it.

7. My colleague Gillian Feeley-Harnik wonders whether such imagery may have arisen within a particular religious tradition, in view of the anticommunionist overtones. The question is a good one. Many of the abolitionists were Quakers; other religious groups in Britain also struggled against the slave trade and slavery. But the stress upon what might be called the "cannibalistic" aspects of sugar-eating also deserves notice.

8. The proslavery faction was quick to respond to such politics, with arguments of their own. Their own propaganda apparatus was brought actively into play. An example turns up in the *European Magazine* for March 1792. There, a writer who dubs himself "Consistency" submits an allegedly authentic letter from a five-year-old boy, reasoning against the moral petition to abstain from sugar in order to save the lives of the slaves.

> Dear Lady L____:
> Forgive me for applying to you to release me from my promise not to drink anything that has Sugar in it. To be sure, I would not wish to have my promise back again, if I was convinced of the truth of what you told me, that every lump of Sugar I put in my mouth, consumed some of the flesh of a poor dead Negro Slave.

The little boy complains of the ridicule to which he was subjected by grownups for persisting in his sacrifice,

> and while they are laughing at me, I see them eating such nice tarts, and cakes, and sweetmeats. . . . Some of the gentlemen told me they had been to the country where the Negroes make Sugar; and that they are never so fat and so happy as when they are making Sugar; and they eat and drink as much as they can; and they love it as much as we do.

Among those who ridiculed him, the boy says, were those who said that the Negroes are engaged in many other activities, such as mining gold and silver, dyeing cloth, cutting trees, and so on. Hence, he reasons, all of the objects produced through their labor are similarly contaminated by slavery. Those who forswear sugar while using mahogany tables and sterling flatware must be hypocrites:

> I cannot think, dear Lady L_____, how anybody who will not eat Sugar because it is eating Negro flesh, can handle gold or silver, or feed themselves with silver spoons or forks; for if eating sugar is eating Negroes flesh, sure every time anybody puts a fork or spoon in their mouths, it is putting a poor dead Negro's finger or toe there. [*European Magazine*, March 1792, 185]

9. Sombart's penchant for targeting groups as the prime movers in the rise of capitalism—Jews and women, for example—rather than studying social systems as systems, made his work less persuasive than it might have been otherwise.

10. Salaman discusses the Solanaceae, which family includes not only potatoes, tomatoes, and peppers, but also tobacco, mandrake, jimsonweed, and the deadly nightshade. European experiences with some of the poisonous plants among the Solanaceae may have made them highly suspicious of potatoes and tomatoes, not to mention the capsicums and tobacco. See Heiser 1969.

11. In his *The Romantic Ethic and the Spirit of Consumerism* [1987], Colin Campbell contends that the capitalist market may satisfy desires, but cannot create them. I think he is only partly right. The capitalist market can take advantage of existing conditions in such a way as to make them appear to define human needs. In the case of a product such as Coca Cola, as I suggested in chapter 2, while the market did not create need, it certainly showed us how it could be bottled.

12. For people interested in how food (in this case, especially sweet food) is linked to this new sort of individual, the film "Eating" offers a particularly brilliant evocation.

13. Some readers may object, on grounds that strong moral commitments about consumption are still being made, commitments that take society and other species fully into account. That is indeed the case; this argument is not intended to ignore or deny it. I mean instead to concentrate on another (and, I think, unfortunately much more powerful) development.

14. Staffan Linder [1970] has dealt imaginatively with the concept of simultaneous consumption. In borrowing his idea to stress the imagined "lack of time" in modern U.S. society, I wrote the following:

> Maximum enjoyment in minimum time has come to mean both divided (simultaneous) consumption—one eats while walking or working, drinks while driving or watching entertainment—and higher frequency of occasions for consumption. Watching the Cowboys play the Steelers, while eating Fritos and drinking Coca-Cola, while smoking a joint, while one's girl sits on one's lap, can be packing a great deal of experience into a short time

and thereby maximizing enjoyment. Or it can be experienced quite differently, depending on the values one holds. [Mintz 1985, 203]

Whatever the case, there is no doubt at all that simultaneous consumption increases consumption; and that is really the point.

15. Figuratively speaking, that is. Just as we are encouraged to suppose that there is no lid on consumption—indeed, that it would be immoral to create one—so, too, we imagine that if we fall, whether from grace or just from economic security, the pit into which we fall may be bottomless. The experience in recent years of many disemployed Americans would suggest that the latter belief, at least, is not entirely misplaced.

6. Color, Taste, and Purity

1. The origin of the term itself is actually still debated. G. Cardona and G. Pellegrini have independently traced the name to the Burmese town of Martaban, just north of Moulmein. The Arabic name is said first to have referred to porcelain ceramics orginating in that town. See Cardona 1969, 34–37; Pellegrini 1976, 92. Some authorities derive the name from a seated figure appearing on a coin; some even suggest that such a figure was used as a mold with which marzipan was formed. But the boundary between historical fact and legend in this regard is dim.

2. Many writers attribute the "invention" of marzipan to the nuns of the Convent of San Clemente, in Toledo. In a period of great hunger— happily coinciding with a plenitude of almonds and sugar!—the nuns hit on the idea of combining ground almonds with the sugar to make a kind of bread: *el pan de San Marcos*, or marzipan. This wildly improbable narrative is recognized by many scholars for what it is, however—the invention of an explanation, not the invention of a sweet.

3. Lorna Sass [1981] has argued that almond milk was popular with the powerful in medieval Europe for medical, religious, and political reasons. However, she gives no examples specific to almonds from the medical literature, and her political argument is simply that the rich chose costly ingredients for their banquet foods. Her view that almond milk could be used as a substitute for cow's milk "on those days when the consumption of cream, milk and eggs was prohibited" [255] is persuasive evidence that almonds were used for religious reasons.

7. Cuisine: High, Low, and Not at All

Arjun Appadurai's 1988 paper on cuisine is the best scholarly article I have ever read on that subject. The only reason for not referring to that paper directly in the text is the wide difference in cultural subject matter. But any reader seriously interested in the subject will find Appadurai's work an ideal place to begin.

1. I am indebted to Nancy Jenkins for pointing this out to me, and for sending me McCarthy's piece.

8. Eating American

1. We Americans—we people of the United States—need to be reminded all of the time that the term "American," which we unconsciously claim as our own, is used by everybody else in this hemisphere. Our neighbors to the south feel with justice that they have an equal claim upon it. Hispanic Americans use the term "North American" to refer to us North Americans, as well as to Canadians. Most Canadians are prepared to call us Americans because they consider themselves Canadians. From here on I will use "American" to mean "North American."

2. The historical literature on North American food and eating is substantial and impressive. A charming place to begin is with Arthur M. Schlesinger's "Food in the Making of America" [1964].

3. A genuine difficulty with my own line of argument is how discouraging—and probably elitist—it may seem to those who truly want to see an American cuisine take shape. It would be easy to conclude that I object to the *idea* of an American cuisine, when in fact I only think it is impossible now to create one. The people who believe we can create a cuisine also believe, and with more reason, that American *cuisines* (in the plural) once existed. No reader of Betty Fussell's *I Hear America Cooking* [1986] can deny the still-visible roots of regional culinary distinction she uncovers. Such works as Damon Lee Fowler's *Classical Southern Cooking* [1995] and Edna Lewis's wonderful *In Pursuit of Flavor* [1988] are eloquent defenses of Southern cuisine. But I do not believe that an American cuisine either preexisted, or has arisen from, regional American cooking. Christopher Kendall, the eloquent publisher and editor of *Cook's Illustrated*, discusses these issues thoughtfully. But I think that his conclusions end up making my point. "It is my belief," he writes:

that at six o'clock in the evening most adult Americans are standing on common ground. We need to get a good dinner on the table, and it makes little difference where we live or who our ancestors were. For better or for worse, we share a modern lifestyle and
therefore share the need for a modern American cuisine. Let's
stop running helter-skelter down the road to diversity, a path that
leads to culinary anarchy. Culinary elitism offers no answers to
our culinary dilemma.

Anyone who doubts the value of a melting-pot cuisine
should consider Thanksgiving, the one holiday most Americans
cherish. In the simplest terms, Thanksgiving is about 240 million
people eating the same menu on the same day. We compare notes
on how the turkey was cooked, on the flakiness of the pumpkin
pie crust, and on the components of the stuffing. It feels good to
share the menu with our neighbors. Despite the abundance on the
table, it's also a meal that has echoes of our ancestral frugality; the
leftovers are eagerly consumed over the long weekend.

As a culture, we gain much from a shared cuisine. It helps to
bind us together in a time when we are constantly being pulled
apart by expressing our individuality. We should heed the lessons
of Thanksgiving. Let's give thanks for our own foods, reflect on
the practical legacy of our culinary past, and then set out to retool
American cooking for the next century. But let's do it together.
We are in desperate need of common ground. [Kendall 1995, 1]

Kendall roots for what we haven't got yet, while telling us we can get
it because we've already got it. I wish I could be convinced that he is
right.

4. See Pimentel and Giampietro 1994a; Giampietro and Pimentel n.d.; Pimentel, Harman, Pacenza, Pecarsky, and Pimentel 1994; Kendall and
   Pimentel 1994; Pimentel and Giampietro 1994b.
5. *New York Times*, April 25, 1995, A23.

Works Cited

Achebe, Chinua. 1973. *Girls at War and Other Stories*. Garden City, N.Y.: Doubleday.

Anonymous. 1777. *An Essay on Tea, Sugar, White Bread . . . and Other Modern Luxuries*. Salisbury, England: J. Hodson.

Appadurai, Arjun. 1988. How to make a national cuisine: Cookbooks in contemporary India. *Comparative Studies in Society and History* 30 (1): 3–24.

Austen, Ralph, and Woodruff Smith. 1990. Private tooth decay as public economic virtue: The slave-sugar triangle, consumerism, and European industrialization. *Social Science History* 14 (1): 95–115.

Austin, Thomas, ed. 1888. *Two Fifteenth Century Cookbooks*. London: N. Trubner.

works cited

Beckford, William. 1790. *A Description of the Island of Jamaica*. 2 vols. London.

Beckwith, Martha. 1928. Notes on Jamaican ethnobotany. *Jamaican Folklore. Memoirs of the American Folk-Lore Society* 21: 1–47. New York: American Folk-Lore Society.

Besson, Jean. 1984. Family land and Caribbean society: Toward an ethnography of Afro-Caribbean peasantries. Pp. 57–83 in *Perspectives on Caribbean Regional Identity*, ed. Elizabeth M. Thomas-Hope. University of Liverpool Monograph Series no. 11.

Boas, Franz. 1921. Ethnology of the Kwakiutl. Thirty-fifth Annual Report of the Bureau of American Ethnology, pp. 57–794. Washington, D.C.: Government Printing Office.

Bourdieu, Pierre. 1984. *Distinction: A Social Critique of the Judgement of Taste*. Cambridge, Mass.: Harvard University Press.

Campbell, Colin. 1987. *The Romantic Ethic and the Spirit of Modern Consumerism*. Oxford and New York: Basil Blackwell.

Cantor, Sidney, and Michael Cantor. 1977. Socioeconomic factors in fat and sugar consumption. Pp. 429–46 in *The Chemical Senses and Nutrition*, ed. M. Kare and O. Maller. New York: Academic Press.

Cardona, G. 1969. Marzapane. *Lingua Nova* 30: 34–37.

Cardoso, Ciro F. S. 1987. *Escravo ou camponês? O protocampesinato negro nas Américas*. Sao Paulo: Editora Brasiliense.

Cassidy, Frederick G., and R. LePage. 1980. *Dictionary of Jamaican English*. 2d ed. Cambridge: Cambridge University Press.

Chance, F. 1762. Treacle. Notes and Queries, 3d ser., Feb. 22: 145–46.

"Consistency." 1792. A Letter to *The European Magazine*, March 1792.

Crane, Eva. 1976. *Honey: A Comprehensive Survey*. London: Heinemann.

Crane, Eva. 1980. *A Book of Honey*. Oxford: Oxford University Press.

Crane, Eva. 1983. *The Archaeology of Beekeeping*. Ithaca: Cornell University Press.

Cundall, Frank, ed. 1939. *Lady Nugent's Journal*. London: The West India Committee.

Curtin, Philip. 1969. *The Atlantic Slave Trade: A Census*. Madison: University of Wisconsin Press.

Dams, L. R. 1978. Bees and honey-hunting scenes in the Mesolithic rock art of eastern Spain. *Bee World* 59 (2): 45–53.

Debien, Gabriel. 1964. La nourriture des esclaves sur les plantations des Antilles françaises aux XVIIè et XVIIIè siècles. *Caribbean Studies* 4 (2): 3–27.

Deerr, Noel. 1949–50. *The History of Sugar*. 2 vols. London: Chapman & Hall.

Elias, Norbert. 1978. *The Civilizing Process*. New York: Urizen Books.

Firth, Raymond. 1957. The place of Malinowski in the history of economic anthropology. Pp. 109–28 in *Man and Culture*, ed. R. Firth. London: Routledge & Kegan Paul.

Forbes, R. J. 1966. *Studies in Ancient Technology*. Vol. 5. Leiden: E. J. Brill.

Fowler, Damon Lee. 1995. *Classical Southern Cooking*. New York: Crown Publishers.

Freeman, Michael. 1977. Sung. Pp. 141–76 in *Food in Chinese Culture*, ed. K.-C. Chang. New Haven: Yale University Press.

Friedman, Jonathan. 1989. The consumption of modernity. *Culture and History* 4: 117–30.

works cited

Fussell, Betty. 1986. *I Hear America Cooking*. New York: Viking.

Genovese, Eugene D. 1972. *Roll, Jordan, Roll*. New York: Random House.

Giampietro, Mario, and David Pimentel. n.d. The tightening conflict: Population, energy use, and the ecology of agriculture. *NPG Forum*, 8 pp.

Goldstein, Judith. 1993. The female aesthetic community. *Poetics Today* 14 (1): 143–63.

Goody, Jack. 1982. *Cooking, Cuisine and Class*. Cambridge: Cambridge University Press.

Gosse, Edmund. 1907. *Father and Son*. New York: Charles Scribner's Sons.

Hall, Douglas. 1988. Planters, farmers and gardeners in eighteenth-century Jamaica. The 1987 Elsa Goveia Lecture. Mona, Jamaica: Department of History, University of the West Indies.

Handler, Jerome S., and Frederick W. Lange. 1978. *Plantation Slavery in Barbados*. Cambridge: Harvard University Press.

Hart, James. 1633. *Klinike or the Diet of the diseases*. London: John Beale.

Heiser, Charles. 1969. *Nightshades: The Paradoxical Plants*. San Francisco: W. H. Freeman.

Hentzner, P. 1757 [1598]. *A Journey Into England*. Strawberry Hill, England.

Higman, Barry W. 1984. *The Slave Populations of the British Caribbean, 1807–1834*. Baltimore: Johns Hopkins University Press.

Hugill, Anthony. 1978. *Sugar and All That . . . a History of Tate & Lyle*. London: Gentry.

Kendall, Christopher. 1995. Common ground. *Cook's Magazine* 13:1.

Kendall, Henry W., and David Pimentel. 1994. Constraints on the expansion of the global food supply. *Ambio* 23 (3): 198–205.

Labarge, Margaret W. 1965. *A Baronial Household of the Thirteenth Century*. London: Eyre & Spottiswoode.

Laurioux, Bruno. 1985. Spices in the medieval diet: A new approach. *Food and Foodways* 1 (1): 43–75.

Lepkowski, Tadeusz. 1968. *Haití*. Vol. 1. Habana: Casa de las Américas.

Le Sage, D. E. 1976. The language of honey. Pp. 426–38 in *Honey: A Comprehensive Survey*, ed. E. Crane. London: Heinemann.

Levey, Martin. 1973. *Early Arabic Pharmacology*. Leiden: E. J. Brill.

Lewis, Edna. 1988. *In Pursuit of Flavor*. New York: Knopf.

Lichtenstein, Alex. 1988. That disposition to theft, with which they have been branded: Moral economy, slave management, and the law. *Journal of Social History* 21 (3): 413–40.

Linder, Staffan. 1970. *The Harried Leisure Class*. New York: Columbia University Press.

Lippmann, Edmund von. 1970 [1929]. *Geschichte des Zuckers*. Nierwalluf bei Wiesbaden: Martin Sandig.

Lopez, Amy. 1948. Land and labour to 1900. *Jamaica Historical Review* 1 (1948): 289–301.

Louis, J. C., and Harvey Z. Yazijian. 1980. *The Cola Wars*. New York: Everest House.

Malinowski, Bronislaw. 1935. *Coral Gardens and Their Magic*. 2 vols. London: George Allen & Unwin.

McKee, Francis. 1991. Ice cream and morality. Pp. 199–205 in *Public Eating: Proceedings of the Oxford Symposium on Food and Cookery*, ed. Harlan Walker. London: Prospect Books.

works cited

Mead, W. E. 1967 [1931]. *The English Medieval Feast*. London: George Allen & Unwin.

Mintz, Sidney W. 1955. The Jamaican internal marketing pattern: Some notes and hypotheses. *Social and Economic Studies* 4 (1): 311–25.

Mintz, Sidney W. 1958. The historical sociology of the Jamaican church-founded free village system. *De West-Indische Gids* 38 (1–2): 46–70.

Mintz, Sidney W. 1961a. Review of Stanley M. Elkins, *Slavery. American Anthropologist* 63 (3): 579–87.

Mintz, Sidney W. 1961b. The question of Caribbean peasantries: A comment. *Caribbean Studies* 1961: 31–34.

Mintz, Sidney W. 1971a. Toward an Afro-American history. *Cahiers d'Histoire Mondiale* 13 (2): 317–32.

Mintz, Sidney W. 1971b. Groups, group boundaries and the perception of race. *Comparative Studies in Society and History* 13 (4): 437–43.

Mintz, Sidney W. 1978a. Was the plantation slave a proletarian? *Review* 2 (1): 81–98.

Mintz, Sidney W. 1978b. Caribbean marketplaces and Caribbean history. *Nova Americana* (1): 333–44.

Mintz, Sidney W. 1982. Choice and occasion: Sweet moments. Pp. 157–69 in *The Psychobiology of Human Food Selection*, ed. Lewis M. Barker. Westport, Conn.: Avi Publishing Company.

Mintz, Sidney W. 1985. *Sweetness and Power*. New York: Viking Penguin Inc.

Mintz, Sidney W. 1989. *Caribbean Transformations*. New York: Columbia University Press.

Mintz, Sidney W., and Douglas Hall. 1960. The origins of the Jamaican internal marketing system. *Yale University Publications in Anthropology* 57: 3–26.

Mintz, Sidney W., and Richard Price. 1992. *The Birth of African-American Culture: An Anthropological Perspective.* Boston: Beacon Press.

Moreau de St. Méry, Médéric-Louis-Élie. 1797. *Description topographique [. . .] de la partie française de l'île Saint-Domingue.* Paris.

Page, Louise, and Berta Friend. 1974. Level of use of sugars in the United States. Pp. 93–107 in *Sugars in Nutrition*, ed. H. L. Sipple and K. W. McNutt. New York: Academic Press.

Paget, Hugh. n.d. The free village system in Jamaica. *Caribbean Quarterly* 1 (4): 7–19.

Pares, Richard. 1960. *Merchants and Planters.* Economic History Review Supplements no. 4. Economic History Society. Cambridge: Cambridge University Press.

Pellegrini, G. 1976. Martabana marzapane. *Lingua Nova* 37: 92.

Pendergrast, Mark. 1993. *For God, Country and Coca Cola.* New York: Charles Scribner's Sons.

Pimentel, David, and Mario Giampietro. 1994a. U.S. population growth threatens irreplaceable farmland. *Clearinghouse Bulletin* 4 (11).

Pimentel, David, and Mario Giampietro. 1994b. Food, land, population and the U.S. economy. Executive summary of a full report by the same title. Commissioned by Carrying Capacity Network, 2000 P St., N.W., Suite 240, Washington, D.C.

Pimentel, David, Rebecca Harman, Matthew Pacenza, Jason Pecarsky, and Marcia Pimentel. 1994. Natural resources and an optimum human population. *Population and Environment* 15 (5): 347–69.

works cited

Pomet, P. 1748. *A Complete History of Drugs*, 4th ed. London.

Price, Richard. 1966. Caribbean fishing and fishermen: A historical sketch. *American Anthropologist* 68 (4): 1363–83.

Ragatz, Lowell J. 1928. *The Fall of the Planter Class in the British Caribbean, 1763–1833*. New York: Appleton-Century.

Revel, Jean-François. 1982. *Culture and Cuisine*. Garden City, N.Y.: Doubleday.

Richards, Audrey. 1932. *Hunger and Work in a Savage Tribe*. London: George Routledge & Sons.

Rozin, Paul. 1987. Sweetness, sensuality, sin, safety, and socialization: Some speculations. Pp. 99–110 in *Sweetness*, ed J. Dobbing. London: Springer Verlag.

Rye, W. B. 1865. *England As Seen By Foreigners*. London: John Russell.

Salaman, Redcliffe N. 1949. *The History and Social Influence of the Potato*. Cambridge: Cambridge University Press.

Sass, Lorna. 1981. The preference for sweets, spices and almond milk in late medieval English cuisine. In *Food in Perspective*, ed. A. Fenton and T. Owen. Edinburgh: John Donald.

Schlesinger, Arthur M. 1964. Food in the making of America. Pp. 220–40 in his *Paths to the Present*. Cambridge: Houghton Mifflin.

Sheridan, Richard. 1974. *Sugar and Slavery*. Baltimore: Johns Hopkins University Press.

Smith, Woodruff. 1992. Complications of the commonplace: Tea, sugar and imperialism. *Journal of Interdisciplinary History* 23 (2): 259–78.

Smith, Woodruff D. 1995. From coffeehouse to parlour: The consumption of coffee, tea and sugar in north-western Europe in the seventeenth and eighteenth centuries. Pp. 148–69 in *Consuming Habits*, ed. Jordan Goodman, Paul E. Lovejoy, and Andrew Sherratt. London: Routledge.

Sombart, Werner. 1967 [1919]. *Luxury and Capitalism*. Ann Arbor: University of Michigan Press.

Spittler, Gerd. 1987. Essen und moral: die Nahrung der Kel Ewey im Alltag und in einer Hungerkrise. *Freiburger Universitätsblätter* 96: 95–111.

Spittler, Gerd. 1993. Lob des einfachen Mahles. Pp. 193–210 in *Kulturthema Essen*, ed. A. Wierlacher, G. Neumann, and H. J. Teuteberg. Berlin: Akademie-Verlag.

Sturtevant, William. 1969. History and ethnography of some West Indian starches. Pp. 177–99 in *The Domestication and Exploitation of Plants and Animals*, ed. P. Ucko and G. W. Dimbleby. Chicago: Aldine.

Trouillot, Michel-Rolph. 1988. *Peasants and Capital: Dominica in the World Economy*. Baltimore: Johns Hopkins University Press.

Tutuola, Amos. 1953. *The Palm Wine Drinkard*. Westport, Conn.: Greenwood Press.

Venner, Tobias. 1620. *Via Recta ad Vitam Longam, or a Plaine Philosophical Discourse*. London.

Warner, Richard, The Rev. 1791. *Antiquitates Culinariae; or Curious Tracts Relating to the Culinary Affairs of the Old English*. London: Blamire.

Wolf, Eric. 1982. *Europe and the People without History*. Berkeley: University of California Press.

Wolf, Eric. 1990. Facing power: Old insights, new questions. *American Anthropologist* 92 (3): 586–96.

Woodham-Smith, Cecil. 1962. *The Great Hunger: Ireland 1845–1849*. London: Hamish Hamilton.

Index

Abd-Ar-Rahman I, 87
Africa, 26, 38, 39, 41, 42, 44, 45, 48, 73, 87, 98, 110
African. *See* Africa
Allspice (*Pimenta officinalis*), 46
Almonds, 15, 86, 87–88, 89, 90
Alsace, 96
Al-Tabassur bi-l-tigara ("Concerning Clarity in Commercial Matters"), 86
Annatto, 39, 47
Anorexia, 5–6, 7
Aquinas, T., 71
Argentina, 109

Artificial sweeteners: aspartame, 53; NutraSweet, 53
Arugula, 116
Australia, 26, 71, 110

Banana (*Musa acuminata*), 11, 39, 44; red, 116
Basil, 116
Beckford, W., 43
Beef, 45, 46, 118, 120
Boas, F., 4, 10
Boston baked beans, 95, 114
Bouillabaisse, 115
Bourdieu, P., 9

index

Bozpopovschini, 76

Brazil, 108; and slavery, 37

Bread, 29, 35, 48, 68, 69, 73, 80, 96, 97, 105, 117; black, 24; white, 24, 89, 118

Breadfruit (*Artocarpus altilis*), 39, 44, 45

Brillat-Savarin, 94

Bulimia, 5, 6, 7

Canada, 39, 71, 108, 109, 110

Capsicums (*C. frutescens, C. annuum*), 39, 46

Captain Bligh, 39

Cardamom, 57

Caribbean, 33, 38–43, 48, 72, 109; diet, 45; slavery, 35, 36, 37; sugar production, 59

Cassava (*Manihot esculenta*), 38, 41, 44

Chance, F., 61

Chicken, 46, 89, 114, 117, 120

Chile, 109

Chinese, 24, 99, 100, 103, 104, 107, 122; agriculture, 103; banquet, 103; cooking, 94, 99

Chocolate, 13, 19, 22, 37, 51, 71

Cinnamon, 56, 57

Clam chowder, 114

Cloves, 56

Coca Cola, 26–28, 30; and World War II, 26, 27

Codfish, 39, 40, 45

Coffee, 19, 22, 25, 26, 37, 39, 42, 51, 71, 77, 83, 120, 121; in Europe, 75

Coke. *See* Coca Cola

Complete History of Drugs, A, 62

Consumer preference, 51, 66

Consumption, 12, 17, 18, 20, 24, 51, 55, 63, 66, 67, 70, 71, 72, 74, 75, 77, 78, 79, 80–81, 82, 87, 118–119, 120, 121, 123–124; mass consumption, 18, 55; and meaning, 7, 13; and power, 12, 13

Coriander, 47, 116

Cornmeal, 38, 40

Costa Rica, 109

Crane, E., 55

Cronin, A. J., 75

Cuba, 26, 37

Cuisine, 15, 31, 38, 42, 44, 45–47, 92, 96, 97–99, 102, 104, 107, 108, 112, 113, 114, 115, 117, 122; African, 38, 44; American, 94, 105, 107, 113, 117; Caribbean, 36, 45; Chinese, 94, 99, 101; defined, 15, 45, 94, 96; European, 56; French, 94, 95, 96; grande or haute, 94, 96, 99–104; Indian, 94; national, 94, 95, 96, 97, 103, 117; regional, 94, 102; slave, 36, 40, 44, 45, 46, 47, 48; Thai, 94

Cultivation, 4, 41; Jamaica, 43, 45; sugar cane, 87

Culture, 21, 23, 34, 36, 40, 107; Afro-American, 48; American, 112; and eating, 93, 94, 103; Japanese, 29; meaning, 21, 23; slave, 36

De Compositione medicamentorum, 60

Deerr, N., 55

Denmark, 109

Diet, 24, 31, 46, 52, 55, 56, 57, 80, 98, 118, 122, 123

Elias, N., 18

England, 57, 59, 61, 71, 111; cane sugar, 76; sucrose, 55

Essay on Tea, Sugar, Whitebread . . . and Other Modern Luxuries, 73

Europe, 12, 39, 55, 56, 75, 87, 98,

108, 109, 110, 115; cuisine, 45; diet, 12; honey, 87; medicine, 60, 88; spices, 46; sugar, 54, 63, 70, 71; sweets, 86, 90

Fasting, 71
Father and Son, 68
Forme of Cury, The, 56, 87
France, 96, 97, 103, 104, 109, 115
Freedom, 13, 14, 33, 34, 36, 37, 47, 124; and food, 13, 35, 47; and slavery, 14, 34, 36, 41, 44; and taste, 14, 33, 34, 36, 37, 47
Freeman, M., 99, 102, 103, 104
Friedman, J., 81, 82, 83
Fuel-economy, 47

Galen, 60, 88
Galenic Theory, 60, 88
George III, 72
Germany, 109, 115
Ginger, 46, 56, 57, 89
Glasgow Herald, 74
Goldstein, J., 81
Gondeshapur (Khuzestan), 60
Goody, J., 98
Gosse, E., 68
Gosse, P., 68, 77
Great Hunger, The, 11

Haiti, 41, 42
Hanway, J., 73, 74
Hart, J., 60, 71
Hatter's Castle, 75
Henry VIII, 55
Hentzner, P., 59
Higman, B., 40, 45
Hippocrates, 60, 88
History and Social Influence of the Potato, The, 11, 76
Hmong, 112
Honey, 14, 50, 53, 55, 58, 60, 62, 63,

64, 65; in alcoholic drinks, 58; in Europe, 55, 56, 86, 87; as medicine, 58, 60–61; perceptions of, 51, 52; as spice, 55, 59; as sweetener, 56; as symbol, 54
Hong Kong, 101
Hot dogs, 90, 113, 114
Hugill, A., 64
Humoral medicine, 60, 88
Hunger, 2, 4, 5, 6, 9, 11, 45
Hunger and Work in a Savage Tribe, 35
Hunt, G., 4

Ice cream, 14, 74, 113
India, 55, 122
Inside meaning, 20, 21, 22, 23, 27, 28, 30, 31
Internal market system, 43
Italy, 96, 97, 104, 109

Jamaica, 39, 41, 42, 43, 45, 46, 59
Japan, 29, 123
Jicama, 116
Joffe, J., 123

Labarge, M. W., 56
Lady Nugent, 46
Le Sage, D. E., 58
Levey, M., 60
Lévi-Strauss, C., 40
Lippmann, Edmund von, 87
Louis, J. C., 27
Lübeck, 90
Lyle, A., 64

McCarthy, M., 98
Mace, 46, 57
McKee, F., 74, 75, 76
Maize (*Zea mays*), 10, 24, 29, 38, 41, 42, 44, 45, 114

Malanga (*Xanthosoma sagittifolium;
   Colocasia esculenta*), 41
Malinowski, B., 4, 10
Mangoes (*Mango indifera*), 39, 44,
   116
Manioc (*Manihot esculenta*), 42
Marshall, G. C., 26
Marx, 29
Marseille, 115
Marzipan, 15, 84, 86, 89–90, 91
Mason, O. T., 10
Mead, 58, 59
Mead, W. E., 57, 87, 88
Mediterranean, 87, 90
Middle East, 39, 54, 70, 87
Milan, 90
Milk, 89, 118, 120; almond, 88, 89,
   90; lactose-free, 116; soy, 116
Molasses, 22, 37, 46, 55, 59, 60, 61,
   62, 64
Moreau de St. Méry, 44
Moryson, F., 59
Murra, J. V., 34

Netherlands, 109
New Zealand, 71
Nigeria, 3
Norway, 109
Notes & Queries, 61
Nutmeg, 46

Outside meaning, 20, 21, 22, 23, 27,
   28, 30

Padre Berlanga, 39
Palm-Wine Drinkard, The, 1
Papaya (*Carica papaya*), 39, 47
Paris, 115
Peanuts (*Arachis hypogaea*), 38
Pendergrast, M., 27
Pepper, 56
Pest Books, 88

Philip the Fair, 89
Pigeon peas, 41
Pimentel, D., 122, 123
Pizza, 113, 114
Plantains, 41, 44, 45
Plantation, 19, 23, 41, 43; economy,
   1; and food, 35; and slavery, 35,
   38, 40, 41, 43, 46; sugar, 1, 90
Pomet, P., 62
Pork, 46, 76, 114, 120
Portugal, 109
Potato, 11, 12, 38, 39, 76, 118; Irish
   potato famine, 11, 12
Power, 12, 13, 18, 27, 28, 29, 30, 31,
   63, 64, 112; and food, 4, 5, 6, 10,
   11, 13, 15, 17–18, 19, 30, 67–68,
   69; and meaning 20, 21, 22, 24;
   personal, 28; of persuasion, 28;
   structural, 22, 29, 30; tactical or
   organizational, 28, 29
Proto-peasants, 42, 43
Puerto Rico, 39, 45, 110

Quinoa, 116

Radicchio, 116
Ragatz, L. J., 72
Revel, Jean-François, 94–95, 102
Rice, 8, 24, 39, 41, 47, 89, 103, 116;
   and the Chinese, 24, 103; and
   the Japanese, 29; and slaves, 47
Richard II, 56, 87
Richards, A., 35
Rozin, P., 77
Rum, 22, 37, 59
Russia, 76, 108

Saffron, 56, 57, 86, 88
Saint Domingue, 44
Salaman, R., 11, 76
Salernum (Sicily), 60
Salt, 40, 45, 57, 80, 88, 118

Santo Domingo, 37

Scotland, 74

Slavery, 14, 22, 33, 34, 39, 40, 41, 44, 47; Caribbean, 35, 36, 37, 48; meaning, 23; slave trade, 22, 23

Slaves, 23, 33–34, 38, 39, 40, 41, 43–44, 48; cooking, 14; food, 36, 37, 38, 43, 47

Sombart, W., 75, 76

Soursop, 116

Spain, 87, 89, 104, 109

Spices. *See individual listings*

Star apples, 116

Sucrose. *See* Sugar

Süddeutsche Zeitung, 123

Sudhoff, C., 88

Sugar, 12, 14, 18–20, 22, 23, 25, 26, 31, 37, 51, 53–56, 59, 62–63, 64, 70–71, 72, 74, 75, 77, 78, 81, 83, 86, 87, 88, 89, 90, 103, 118, 119; beet, 51; cane, 50, 51, 76, 87; and Coca Cola, 26; and honey, 14, 51, 52, 55, 58, 60, 65; maple, 51; meaning, 14; as medicine, 60, 61, 88; and morality, 67, 71, 73, 76, 77, 79; and power, 12, 13; purity, 15, 89; and slavery, 73, 76; as spice, 56–58, 59; as sweetener, 50, 55; whiteness, 15; and working class, 18, 19

Sweden, 109

Sweetness and Power, 18

Sweet potatoes, 41, 44, 45

Syrup, 60, 65, 88, 100; Golden, 64; high-fructose corn, 51; in medicine, 60, 61

Taiwan, 100

Taro (*Colocasia esculenta*), 39, 41, 44

Tea, 18, 19, 20, 23, 31, 62, 63, 71, 72, 73, 74, 75, 78, 103; and British, 20, 22, 23, 65; in Europe, 12; and working class, 18

Tobacco, 20, 26, 37, 63, 71, 76, 78, 83; in England, 18, 19, 22

Toledo (Spain), 60

Treacle, 61, 62; as sweetener, 60

Tuber (*Calathea allouia*), 1

Turkey, 104

Turmeric, 47

Tutuola, A., 1, 2

Two Fifteenth-Century Cookbooks, 88

Über den Luxus, 75

United States, 7, 10, 14, 15, 37, 52, 108, 109, 110, 111, 118, 122, 123; cuisine, 94, 114, 115; honey, 51; sugar, 50; sweeteners, 53

Uruguay, 109

Venner, T., 60

War, 4, 14, 26, 27, 28, 31, 52, 53, 109, 123; and food choice, 25, 26; Spanish American, 110; World War II, 13, 25, 26, 110, 111, 119

Whiteness, 15, 89; and purity, 15, 89, 90

Wine, 1, 12, 59, 95, 98

Wissler, C., 10

Wolf, E., 22, 28, 29, 30

Woodham-Smith, C., 11

Yam, 4, 39, 42

Yazijian, H. Z., 27